THE WAR
AS I
SAW IT

THE WAR
AS I
SAW IT

IN RHODESIA, NOW ZIMBABWE, THROUGH THE EYES OF A BLACK BOY

GEORGE MAKONESE MATUVI

WOLSAK
& WYNN

Published by Wolsak and Wynn Publishers
280 James Street North
Hamilton, ON L8R2L3
www.wolsakandwynn.ca

Editor: Noelle Allen | Copy editor: Peter Midgley
Cover and interior design: Jen Rawlinson
Cover image: Helicopter in Victoria Falls in Zimbabwe in Africa © Mara Duchetti
Author photograph: George Makonese Matuvi
Typeset in Adobe Caslon Pro and Gin
Printed by Brant Service Press Ltd., Brantford, Canada

10 9 8 7 6 5 4 3 2 1

 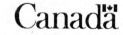

The publisher gratefully acknowledges the support of the Canada Council for the Arts and the Ontario Arts Council. We also acknowledge the financial support of the Government of Canada through the Canada Book Fund and the Government of Ontario through the Ontario Book Publishing Tax Credit and Ontario Creates.

Library and Archives Canada Cataloguing in Publication

Title: The war as I saw it : in Rhodesia, now Zimbabwe, through the eyes of a Black boy / George Makonese Matuvi.
Names: Matuvi, George Makonese, author.
Identifiers: Canadiana 20230497152 | ISBN 9781989496695 (softcover)
Subjects: LCSH: Matuvi, George Makonese. | LCSH: Matuvi, George Makonese—Childhood and youth. | LCSH: Matuvi, George Makonese—Family. | LCSH: Zimbabwe—History—Chimurenga War, 1966-1980—Personal narratives. | LCGFT: Personal narratives. | LCGFT: Autobiographies.
Classification: LCC DT2990 .M38 2023 | DDC 968.91/04092—dc23

I dedicate this book to my father who passed away in 2002.

My brothers and sisters and I are so grateful for the life lessons that my father and mother gave to us.

My mother is one of the most resilient people I have ever known. It's because of her strong nurturing and love for each of my siblings, her nine children, that we survived.

CONTENTS

This book describes a true story of the war that I saw as a young boy and how it affected my family. All my father ever wanted was to provide his kids, us, with a good education, food and shelter.

INTRODUCTION

This book is about my life growing up during the War of Liberation in the southern African country of Zimbabwe, formerly known as Rhodesia.

My father was a small businessman in a rural area in the Midlands province of Zimbabwe, a small place called Chamini, near the town called Zvishavane. It is surrounded by mountains and a river called the Runde wiggles through the steep topography into our valley. The river and the mountains serve many purposes in this remote area: people fish in the river, bathe in it, grow gardens next to it and get their fresh drinking water from it. The mountains serve as a space for feeding the cattle and as a source of various fruits – from guavas to an assortment of wild berries. As a child, a day trip to the mountains to bring back the cattle was an adventure not to miss. Now living near one of the major cities in Canada, I begin to realize why all the young boys always wanted to go up to the mountains. Whenever I have gone back to Chamini, I have not been able to go back to the mountains, but as I looked at them, I could visualize the winding paths running through the valleys and over the mountainside. Even now, I can remember a beautiful spring oozing from the ground where people and animals could not pass without a sip of fresh water. The water seeping from that aquifer is probably the best I have ever tasted.

In my memories going up the mountains and spending the day out there was special. We always had a plan. We would go early to find the cattle then slowly make our way home. We would stop to climb the wild fruit trees, pull fruit straight from the branches and eat the juicy sour fruit called matamba, Natal oranges as they are called in English, or we'd stop by a boy-high bush with fresh fruit called nhengengi, sour plums. I always tell people if you go to Africa do not go and stay in some fancy hotel all the time – go to the rural areas. This is where you see life from a different angle; you feel it, literally taste it. This is where time is measured by the amount of sunlight or moonlight. Time slows down for you, as if the entire world is yours to enjoy. At least that's how it felt when I was growing up there, in my early childhood years.

This is also a place where you realize that this universe is huge. Looking out into the sky at night with no artificial lights around, you can see every little star, shooting stars, strange formations of stars and the dark corners, which your eyes cannot see the furthest edges of in the sky. Tiny flickering green and red lights from planes flying thousands of feet above the earth appear now and then. You begin to understand that even darkness is important sometimes, the land below your feet starts to cool off as the night progresses towards the inevitable approach of morning. Your thoughts start to wander in a calm way; you begin to think about nothing. You ask yourself what it all means and you cannot wait to see the sun again in the morning and enjoy the day and the sunset again.

Sunsets in Chamini are absolutely breathtaking as the sun looks like it's sitting on top of the mountains and a shadow from the mountains is cast on the valley below, almost as if warning you that it's time to go home for dinner. In this area most people do not care to have watches; the position of the sun tells you the time. As I was growing up, the sun setting meant it was time to gather the cattle; a signal to start herding your cattle home to the kraal.

With the arrival of the war my family lost everything, including our feeling of tranquility and our sense of purpose. Our lives were changed forever. Many in Zimbabwe still suffer even now as a result of the war. Liberation is always tricky. Who does the liberating and what are the effects of the war on the children and families? These effects can spread across generations, as I witnessed growing up. While I now live in Canada, every time I go to Zimbabwe, I see families whose lives still bear the scars of the war, having lost their son, father, sister or other relative during it. War does not only affect those who are directly exposed to it, it impacts them and their families for years to come.

CHAPTER 1
WAR ARRIVES

Hidden in this quiet mountainous area my father, Cleophas Kira Makonese, built a little store for the community. In the store he sold everything from bread, sugar and clothes to manual farm implements such as hoes and plows. He also sold corn seeds for the locals to farm their staple food. The store was situated next to the school, which was also a gathering point for the community. My father had two wives, Jesslin and Esnati Makonese, and several rural farming fields to sustain our huge family. He had gone to school up to the equivalent of a second year in high school today. During his time he could have been a teacher, but he chose to be a small businessman. My mom, Esnati, his first wife, was a very hard-working woman who helped him to set up his business in a place that is now named after him – KwaMakonese.

On the day the war arrived, I was playing keep-ups with my

brother Paul using our homemade soccer ball in the yard. Soccer was the most popular game that young boys played in Zimbabwe when I was a child. The ball was normally made of a collection of plastic bags rolled together into the shape of a ball. Plastic grocery bags formed the inside of the ball and the outer plastic bag was normally from a mealie-meal bag, which was slightly thicker and could withstand the kicking much better than the grocery bags. Mealie-meal is ground corn, used to make the staple food called sadza. In the olden days people used to grind the corn on a piece of stone, crushing the corn between two rocks, causing the dry corn shells to break apart and form a kind of coarse flour. The flour was poured slowly into a pot of boiling water and gently stirred into a thin porridge. Nowadays people go to a grinding mill where pulverizing the corn takes a matter of minutes. But you can also just buy the already made cornmeal from a shop in plastic bags ranging from ten to fifty kilograms. We used to make our soccer balls from a twenty-kilogram empty mealie-meal bag. It was just the right size to fit enough plastic bags inside it to make a ball.

This homemade ball did not bounce very well and it took some getting used to to control it. It was heavy and did not go extremely far when you kicked it, but I tell you it brought a lot of joy for most kids in the rural areas. You only got to kick a genuine leather ball when you started school. Normally the school had one or two leather balls that were used by the school team and the best way to get to kick a real ball was when the school team was practising. The younger kids would hang around the goalpost area waiting for the ball to be kicked off the football pitch out of play. Since there were no nets, the ball normally flew through and as young kids we would run to pick it up for the older students playing on the team. Once the ball was in hand, we kicked it as hard as possible back to the players in the field. That was our only way to feel a real soccer ball. Soccer is my favourite game, I could go on and on talking about my love for soccer, but on this day it was different. This day the course of my life was changed forever.

My mother was preparing dinner. Normally we ate sadza as the main course with sour milk and some boiled fresh corn and vegetables. This was not sour cream, this was fresh milk from the cow, which had been left out for about a week, that way it started to separate, and the water went to the bottom, while the thick cream stayed up in the jar. The locals call it "mukaka wakakora." Boiled corn, roasted corn and cornmeal porridge – it was always corn something, since corn was our staple food. Though in Zambia the sort-of-sadza thick porridge is made from cassava.

The sun was almost leaning on the mountain's side and outside it was still ridiculously hot when I saw the line of heavily armed men approach our home. I froze on my feet. This was my first time to cast my eyes on the so-called freedom fighters. The Comrades were known by the villagers as "Vana" or "Vana-vevhu," meaning Children of the Earth. Their guns were hanging from their shoulders and some had guns on their backs. Some were even carrying two guns on their backs and at the back of the line one of them was carrying this long cylindrical weapon, which I later learned was called a bazooka or RPG, meaning rocket-propelled grenade. The weapons were of assorted colours, shapes and sizes, and ranged from AK-47 to FN rifles, but many of the guns had these curly bullet holders.

The freedom fighters used anything they could lay their hands on. They even used FN rifles that they took from the fallen Rhodesian forces. They would take away the weapons from their enemies after they killed them in a battle and they would store the weapons in mountain caves, carrying whatever guns they could on them. Sometimes the freedom fighters would get the locals to wrap the weapons up in plastic bags and bury them in cornfields for storage.

Our home was a principal place in our village. It was where the school was and where my father's store was, which was the only store in a twenty-kilometre radius.

My father hastily stood up in surprise and horror. I saw the fear on his face and I knew then and there that this was not good. Time froze for me; the gap between my father and my brother and I playing with the soccer ball was too big for me to run to him. The freedom fighters were very fast; they surrounded the home quickly and I soon found myself face to face with a heavily armed man who was greeting me, smiling at me. I could not smile back. He gestured for me to kick the ball to him, but I was confused and just held the ball in my hand. I remember him saying, "Give it your best shot, kick it hard." I kicked the ball towards him and he kicked it back and stopped, staring at me with a big grin on his face. He asked me to kick again, gesturing with his swinging motion as he threw the ball back to me. I kicked the ball again, this time harder, and he said, "That's more like it." Then he started talking about the national soccer team.

I could not seem to get myself to listen. I was in shock and fear and so he eventually moved on to the end of the yard of our home, facing the forest to look for intruders. His movements were quick and I could see him watching from side to side, sort of scanning the area. It was weird to see him moving around with all the guns and equipment he was carrying.

Not knowing what was going on outside, my mother yelled for me to come in to the kitchen, a hut in the centre of the yard. After waiting for a few minutes and wondering what was going on outside, since it was common that if she called that dinner was ready we would be there in seconds, she shouted again and this time as she shouted, she came out of the kitchen.

She was met at the door by a gun barrel to her face. The soldier was not actually pointing his gun at her, he had just swung his gun in her direction as he turned to look at her. I was scared and confused, not knowing what was going to happen. I thought the freedom fighter was going to shoot her. Time seemed to stop again. My mum yelled, "Mai hwe, Mai hwe!"

The freedom fighter then spoke rapidly. "Mai mushatya henyu," he said. It means "Mother, do not be scared," and he continued to say everything is okay. He sat down by the door of the hut and started talking to her, trying to calm her down.

My mother was visibly shaking as she looked over and saw her husband surrounded by gunmen. The freedom fighter repeated himself several times, telling my mum not to be scared, but with no success. My mum sat down, breathing heavily and sobbing in horror, with her hands to her head. I feared for her and for all of us. I could not do anything for my mum or dad or for me. The freedom fighter asked what she was cooking, trying to calm her down and said that they were all hungry. Then he told her that they wanted to talk to my father first.

The men introduced themselves as the Vanavevhu, the Children of the Earth. They asked my father to sit back down and one of the freedom fighters put his gun down. He explained to my father that they were there to liberate all the povo, the people. They told him the war had now arrived in the area and that increasing numbers of the Vanavevhu would arrive from that day on. My father was told that he would be required to support the struggle for liberation. They demanded goods from the store that they did not pay for, but there was no choice. This was the minute that changed my life forever, the turning point of my childhood. I believe the person I am today has a lot to do with that moment.

The freedom fighter talked to my father for about half an hour, though it seemed like an awfully long time to me. One of the men came over to where we were standing and asked for our names, grade in school and how school was. I do not know what I said to him; it did not matter that much at that time. I was very scared. I know he was trying to make us feel relaxed, but there is one thing I learnt during the war: you can never relax if someone carrying a gun is standing close to you, whether it's pointed at you or not. However, it is a completely different feeling when the gun is pointed at you, as I learnt a few months later.

I had heard a lot of stories about the Vanavevhu, how they beat up people and, in some cases, killed people if they suspected that they were a "sellout." It was a weird feeling, standing there as my brain whirled, wondering what was going to happen to my parents, our family. My mother had been ordered back into the kitchen and a soldier stood by the door. I continued standing there as the soldier talked to my father. After some time he gave a hand signal to the other freedom fighters and the gunmen disappeared into the bushes as quickly as they had arrived. They moved so smoothly it looked as if the forest swallowed them, as if the forest and soldiers were one.

By now it was getting dark. I could hear cowbells ring and echo between the mountains as older boys brought back the cattle from the grazing areas. My father was talking to my mother in the kitchen and from the way they were talking I could sense there was more trouble to come. My father was whispering and using very subtle and minimized hand gestures. I could see him leaning into my mother's face, making sure that we children could not hear what he was saying. However, even if you were a baby you could have picked up that he was scared too.

Growing up I had never actually seen my father scared. The fear you feel as a child when the person that protects you is scared is intense. It felt like something in the air had snuffed out the happiness in our home. I followed my father to the shop. As we walked, I asked who those people were, if they were going to come back and kill us. At that moment my father turned around and looked at us, the children who crowded around him: my sister Evelyn, also known as Tadzidza (which means "We have learnt" in Shona); my brothers Paul, Sydney, Wilmore and Tomson; and myself. We stayed at home with my mother all the time, while the older siblings were away in boarding school at Dadaya High School. He realized that we were all standing there waiting for an answer and that we were more scared than he was. Then my father smiled and said no, we just must be more careful now, the war was getting closer to our area. He said the freedom fighters were going to stay in the mountains and that they would not bother us. He told us they said they were here to free everyone. It did not make sense to me. Free us from who or what? Our lives as I knew it were very nice. I did not understand. He told us not to worry.

As night fell my father disappeared into the store carrying empty boxes. From the clothing section he took all the men's jeans, shirts and pants and put them into one box. All the cigarettes, toothpaste and candy bags went in another.

The Vanavevhu wanted food, clothing, cigarettes and pain-killers such as Cafenol, a common headache medication and painkiller at the time. They had ordered my father to put all these items in boxes and bring them to the Runde River. Since this was my father's very first time to be in contact with the freedom fighters, he took his battered Datsun and drove to the location that was close to the Runde River. When he got there, there was no one in sight. He turned off the engine and switched off the truck lights. Suddenly the whole area was pitch-black under the canopy of thick vegetation along the river. My father could hear the loud sounds of the frogs and other nightly creatures. There was no one in sight. Then suddenly my father heard footsteps coming from all around him as the freedom fighters surrounded my father from all directions.

The leader was terribly upset with my father. He told him that he could get all of them killed. I remember my father telling us the story many a time, repeating the man's words, "You bring your truck here, making all this noise to our base! Never do that again or we will shoot you and burn your truck."

My father quickly learnt these guys meant business. One time they would be nice and then suddenly you did something they did not like and they could kill you. The base was a meeting place that the freedom fighters chose in the woods. They would come during the day and check out the place to make sure they could escape if a battle broke out. In most cases, all the Vanavevhu would escape and the locals would be the ones who would get caught or killed at the base.

The freedom fighters quickly took the stuff from the truck and my father was told to drive back with no headlights in the night, to only use moonlight. The moon was not up yet but my father drove all the way from the river on a winding dirt path not big enough to be a road. He was also told that when he got home, he was to come back to the base for further instructions. When he got to the house, he said goodbye to us as if he was not coming back again. He was not crying but you could hear from his voice that this was serious. When my parents had serious things going on my father always addressed my mother with "Mai Wiribeti," which means Wilbert's mum. It is a custom in that part of the world that a wife is addressed as the mother of the first son or daughter. My father said to my mother that the war that they had been hearing about was finally here.

Stories of the freedom fighters having been seen in the woods had been talked about frequently. One story was that a strange looking group of people were seen very close to our home at dusk days before this unexpected visit. Apparently, this was true and now they had arrived. The freedom fighters were known to check out a place first from afar, using binoculars to see who lived there and sometimes count how many people lived there.

My father walked back to the base that night, where he was made to sit on the ground behind a tree with the leader of the freedom fighters. He was eating, but he immediately told my father that there were many more groups coming and the war would be in our area soon. He said the freedom fighters were going to liberate everyone from the hands of the Rhodesian government. As you can imagine, if you tell a poor person that things are going to change for the better, the message was good news and it gave people hope that their lives would change for the better. The Comrades had a tendency of embellishing the benefits of fighting the war for the people. In some cases, they told people that they were going to take over all the soldiers' trucks after they won the war and give the trucks to the people for carrying cow manure for fertilizing their fields.

It was like music to the ears of the poor people. These promises were like bringing rural people to heaven and offering whatever heaven looks like. Most of the people believed the promises. My father had been singled out as the smart one, and of course in that part of the rural area a person with a little grocery store, educated to standard six and owning a truck was important. He brought the people the necessities they needed from town, such as salt, sugar, cooking oil, bread, farming implements and clothing. But my father also realized that some people would not have the money to pay and so he also bartered with the locals, taking dry buckets of corn in exchange for salt, which he then bagged in jute bags and sold to Grain Marketing Board for real cash. He used that money to order the necessities that people needed in the store.

A lot of the information the freedom fighters told the locals was explained during pungwe sessions, which were all-night rallies. The pungwe sessions were geared towards maximizing support from the people. Supporters were promised that after the war, they would take over everything. The people were promised that they would go to the towns and have whatever they wished from the shops, people were promised that they would take over farms. My father was promised that all his business losses caused by supplying the freedom fighters with food and clothing taken from the store would be repaid. My father was promised money, lots of money, from the new people's government and assistance from the government to get his business back.

The people were promised that after the war they would have good roads and electricity would be brought to the rural areas and that rich people would be forced to share their wealth. All these promises made the locals more supportive of the freedom fighters. They cooked them food whenever they showed up, which most of the time was in the middle of the night. People took turns to kill their only form of wealth, their livestock – their goats and cattle – for fresh meat to feed the freedom fighters.

The Vanavevhu took clothes from the people, such as jeans and shoes. If they saw someone wearing a nice jacket, they would sweet-talk you into exchanging clothes, as most of their clothes would be in bad condition. It felt good for some of the locals for it felt like exchanging clothes was a direct connection with the freedom fighters. In some cases, the Vanavevhu would exchange their tattered and torn clothes and take better clothes, especially dark-coloured clothes, from the young men.

In the cold season they asked for blankets from the locals, which they rolled up and carried on their backs. Sometimes they would leave the blankets behind and the locals would go back the next day and pick up the blankets. People were also asked to take care of the wounded freedom fighters. If a group had someone extremely sick or they had wounded fighters, they would come into an area at night, wake up people, ask for the chief of the area to appoint someone to take care of the wounded and then leave the wounded Comrades there. If a freedom fighter was killed, they would ask the locals to bury the fallen freedom fighter. A select group of elders would be asked to give the freedom fighter a respectful burial. Everything happened at night.

Dark jeans were the freedom fighters' favourite type of clothing because the pants were more durable. I remember the day that my father was asked to give away all the jeans he had in the store. The Vanavevhu showed up just after the sun went down. They arrived with the nightfall and they seemed to appear from all directions. It took them less than five minutes to surround our home, then two guys went into the store with my dad and came out with boxes of merchandise – from the popular Super Pro sneakers and canned beef to clothes and blankets. I grew up at the back of the shop and my father had taught us to be vigilant when working the store and not to give away stuff. We always had to make sure that people paid for something before we handed them the item. At this point I felt that the freedom fighters were stealing from my family.

The soldiers tried to make jokes with us kids. I was not sure if my father was going to resist and shout at the freedom fighters this time, for I knew with all the stuff they were taking that my father would not be able to order more goods. Besides the food we grew in the fields, the store was our family's only means of getting extra money. Without that there was no way to replenish the goods taken from the store. Before they left, the Comrades sat with my father, swearing that people like him would be recognized after the war as heroes. But that never happened. The promises they spread to the people assured them of food and information about the whereabouts of the Rhodesian forces. My father was promised time and time again that he would be given money to replace his goods after the war was over.

Some of the promises were used to recruit young men who would be sent for training on how to use a gun and possibly be deployed to a different area to fight the guerrilla battles. The promise for the young recruits was better lives, jobs and money.

The name for the battles, "guerrilla warfare," was used by the Rhodesian forces because the freedom fighters did not have a defined location where they operated from; they moved around in the forest and attacked the soldiers suddenly. The Rhodesian forces could not figure out where they lived. In most cases the Rhodesian forces were ambushed as they moved around in the rural areas. The locals had little information of the whereabouts of the freedom fighters. Vanavevhu groups rarely revealed where they were headed and they regularly tricked people by telling them incorrect information about their next destination. When crossing rivers, they would choose rocky areas with no sand to avoid leaving footprints. There is a story about a guy who used to repair their shoes . . . The story was that around ten of them came to his home and asked him to glue soles on their shoes facing backwards so that their footprints would show them going the opposite direction.

I remember one time when my father was asked to take care of a group that had been food poisoned. Many of the fighters from that group died, but a few remained. The group leader, who was extremely popular in the area and who regularly visited my father at night, was one of the survivors. When his group got poisoned, he came to our home in the middle of the night, banging on the door frantically. He asked to speak to my father privately outside at the back of the house. He told my father that members of his group were dying, that he had already lost a few and he himself was extremely sick. He asked my father to go to the nearest town, Zvishavane, which was known during that time as Shabani, and get him some medications. On a piece of paper, he wrote what he wanted. Rumour has it that he had been a doctor before joining the group. My father did not know how he could get the medications, but he had to find a way. If he did not, he risked the whole family's chance for survival.

My father had one distant relative who was a doctor at a hospital in Zvishavane. He went and begged for medication from him. He told the doctor if he did not get the medication that the family would be in danger. The doctor gave him some of the medications. The poisoned freedom fighters stayed in hiding by the riverside where they could get fresh water.

When my father came back the leader was now seriously ill, but he refused to stay in anyone's home. He took the medications and told my father the secret location in the thick bush where he would be hiding and told the chief to ask someone to bring him food daily. The poisoned fighter stayed in the bush near the river for a couple of weeks until he recovered. This man came back years after the war to thank my father for saving his life. The last I heard, he contacted one of the family years after my father passed away, still expressing his gratitude for my father saving him from a near-death experience.

During the time he was hiding in the bush, the recovering fighter read books. My older brother was tasked with finding him books. My father always travelled with my big brother, who was old enough to drive. He drove the car most of the time and my father would sit as a passenger. My brother told me one of his tasks was to find books and alcohol for the freedom fighters.

Among the Vanavevhu there were some educated fighters who read and spoke very good English. I was told there were also some fighters who were doctors who knew how to take care of the wounded. These educated fighters helped in strategizing attacks and they had the real information about how the war was going. Some information was passed along via letters. If a group visited the area, they could leave a letter or send a letter to another group. Young men called "mujiba" would be sent with the message to another village to leave it for another group of freedom fighters who would be coming through. This whole process was very secret – only a trusted few knew about the path the information followed.

Vanavevhu did not have cars but there were stories of them asking for people's cars and hitching a lift during the night to travel long distances to be dropped off somewhere far away. The Rhodesian forces would put up roadblocks during the day so the story of them asking someone to drive them at night is plausible. I just could not see them walking from Maputo in Mozambique, where most of them trained, to reach the middle of the country. However, the freedom fighters pushed the story that they walked all the way on foot. I would agree that they walked in their areas of operation by foot, but it's hard to imagine they had walked all the way around the whole country by foot.

When the war was at its peak, it was clear that they were recruiting young men directly from the local areas and those who were recruited locally did not go to Mozambique. The new recruits were trained somewhere in the mountains. It was more like on-the-job training according to some who returned after the war – mostly how to use a gun. The bulk of the local recruits were used by Vanavevhu for carrying their gear and for navigating the local forest. For that they would be accepted into the group and be given a gun. Once recruited, they would not go back home. The freedom fighters stayed on mountaintops where they could watch the valley below. Most of the settlements in rural areas are in the valleys or along the dirt roads that cut across the area, winding through the villages.

My village was surrounded by hills and a couple of mountains and there was a dirt road that cut across the valley, running in the narrow opening of the mountains. If you were up a hill or mountain and a car was driving on this dirt road, you could see the plume of dust behind the vehicle. Sometimes you could see the plume of dust before you even heard the sound. This used to amaze me when I was young – until I did physics and learnt about the speed of sound and the Doppler effect. Using binoculars, Vanavevhu would identify the vehicle from the top of the hill.

One day just before dusk the Rhodesian forces were driving along the road, deploying soldiers into parts of the villages. Unaware that they were being watched, they were fired upon by an RPG-7 launcher. It was the Comrades' common method to hit the leading vehicle, crippling the convoy. Then they would shoot into the chain of army trucks using rapid-fire rifles, the most common of which was the AK-47. The thud and boom from the RPG were felt in the ground and the sound of the RPG echoed off the mountains. For me it was as if the explosion was a few feet away.

I ran into the kitchen hut where my mother was already pouring water to extinguish the fire where she was cooking. It was common that if the Rhodesian forces got to a home and found a fire burning in the kitchen, they would take the log of fire and use it to burn the huts. The Rhodesian forces knew that villagers were feeding the freedom fighters. The villagers had no choice, whether they liked it or not. The freedom fighters had guns.

We lay down on the floor while the gunfight went on. The sound of the gunfire reverberated through the valley and the ground. I could hear and feel the thud of the rocket as it was fired again. After fifteen minutes or so there was silence. By this time it was already dark and my mother whispered for us to get up as she peeped outside to see if anyone was coming. My mom, four of my siblings and I hurried out quietly. I was scared. My father was not at home on this day. In the moment of fear sometimes the bushes looked like a person and I gripped my mother's hand tightly as we moved in the dark. We did not follow the path – we walked across the field into the stubby bushes at the edge of the yard. We walked in the opposite direction from where the gunfire had erupted. It was quiet, but we could see the smouldering fire of the burning army truck from a distance. Then there were several explosions as the truck burnt. I assume it was ammunition and possibly fuel from the burning truck.

There was no time to lock up or check anything; as we got out of the yard we started walking rapidly, almost running. If it was during the day, we could have been running but during the night we needed to keep close to our mom to not lose her. She kept looking around to make sure we were all there. I could only go as fast as my mother's brisk half-running walk. We headed for the mountains. The gunfire erupted again and, as I turned to look in the direction of the sound, I could see the specks of red bullets coming off of one side of the mountains and the other side of the adjacent hill.

We briskly walked-ran for about an hour. There was no time to feel tired. In fact, we did not even think about it. We had to go as far as we could. Suddenly a roaring sound came out of the opening between the two mountains. We could see a bright searchlight in the sky from the helicopter in the area where the fighting was coming from. As the helicopter circled the area there was another boom from an RPG-7. I took it that the freedom fighters were now shooting at the helicopter. We continued to run towards the mountain as more gunfire sporadically erupted.

By the time we reached the first house beside the mountains, the gunfire had stopped. We frantically entered the yard of a chief called Vaswondo at the beginning of the next village, whose house was one of the last houses before you entered the mountains. We noticed it was deserted and we carried on to the next house, Baba Morgan's house. After a few minutes of briskly walking, we entered Baba Morgan's yard and knocked on the door. It was quiet for a moment and then suddenly the front door cracked open. A stocky, grey-haired man opened the door and he waved for us to come in. We went in quickly and he shut the door behind us. Inside, his whole family was sitting quietly. We huddled in the corner with the other kids as my mother whispered to Baba Morgan's wife. Baba Morgan braced the door with anything he could find. There were no lights; the room was dark. By this time, it was late in the night and we sat there tired from the running and rapid walking, but I kept my eyes open and listened for any sounds from outside. I do not know how I fell asleep or at what time; the room was so quiet that it was hard to even hear the sound of breath.

I woke up at dawn to the normal sounds of cowbells as the cattle were just starting to move around. I realized all the adults were already outside. I looked over to where my mum had been sitting through the night, but she and Mai Morgan were already outside making a fire in the mud hut kitchen. I got up and woke up my brother and we went to find our mother.

My mother told us we could not go back to our house or shop yet. She told us no one knew if the Rhodesian forces had left the area. If we went back, we would be a target and could get killed or captured. We spent the day there and Baba Morgan went over to check the situation later on. He passed by the shop and the school to check if anything had happened.

He came back and reported that all was normal and that he had heard the fighting was going in the other direction from our area, but he suggested we should stay for a day for things to settle.

The next day we cautiously went back to our house. Some people believed that the war had chased the Rhodesian forces out of the area and that they were now scared to come back. We knew it was just a matter of time. They would come back and possibly another battle would happen because the Vanavevhu loved the mountains around our village. It made it difficult for someone to ambush them except by air. There were rumours the freedom fighters were now occupying all the surrounding mountains. There was also a rumour that they considered this area to be safe for them, therefore if they fought battles somewhere they would come to these mountains afterwards and spend some days in safety.

However, as fighting went on day after day, our family, and my father specifically, became a target. We heard a rumour that he was now being looked for by the Rhodesian soldiers. One afternoon after church a loud rumble of noise came from the dirt road. I could see a plume of dust in the distance. People who were coming out of church ran in different directions. In a matter of minutes the whole congregation had disappeared, running away to their homes or into the bush. This was our home, so my father told us to go to the back of the house and stay there. My mother took us all into the back of the store, which was attached to our house, while my father and big brother remained in the front entrance to the store.

As the sound of the army trucks grew louder and louder, I sat there thinking this was the time when we would be packed into the trucks and taken for torture. I could hear the trucks come to a halt with the loud puffing of the brakes. I then heard a lot of footsteps as the soldiers surrounded the house. The door flew open from a kick from one the soldiers. Two them came in in full military gear, their guns pointing in all directions as they ordered us to get out of the house. As we left, three soldiers went into the house with their guns cocked and ready to fire.

As they were searching the house, one of them shouted to my mother, "Is there anybody else in the house?"

My mother replied, "No!" I could hear the fear in my mother's voice. We were all scared.

My father was called out of the store and into the yard, where he was asked several questions about the freedom fighters: When last did you see them? How many were they? Which direction did they go? The most frightening moment was when the interrogator said to my father, "We found some remains of canned beef, empty cigarette packets and empty soft drink bottles and we know that there is no other store in these parts. We know that these items came from your store and one person has already told us that you are supplying the terrorists with all sorts of help."

I will always remember my father looking at the soldier as he replied, "Now listen, young man, what do you want me to do? I settled here so I could farm and have a small store to feed my family, but you guys come in here brandishing your guns and ask me questions; the terrorist freedom fighters come here with their guns too and they want stuff from my store . . . Can I say no? Can you say no if someone has a gun in his hand?"

The soldier looked at my father for a second and he said, "I can kill you right now, old man, and not one question will be asked. Do not give them anything."

My father looked at the soldier and said, "You can kill me right now. I am ready. What do you guys want me to do? I told you they have guns, just like you. It does not matter who kills me. You can kill me, or they can kill me."

I remember my father shouting at the soldiers, "Please shoot me! Kill me now, in front of my family, you cowards, or get out of my home and look for the terrorists in the bush."

At that point the soldier stood up and said, "We are watching you, old man. Today I will let you go but when I return, I will burn your house and kill your family and your little terrorist friends." Then the soldier turned around to us and said, "Your father is stubborn." He said to my mother, "Mother, tell him to stop giving stuff to the terrorists." The soldier was now pacing around my father. "Can you not see the terrorists are going to lose? They have no transport. They have to walk to every place. Sooner or later, you are going to run out of food so you will not be able to supply them and they will kill you and they won't have any food so they will give up. You and your family are going to die for nothing!" After that the soldiers hurried into their trucks and left.

Then things started to get even more tricky for my father. Someone reported to the Vanavevhu that he was seen talking to the Rhodesian forces and giving them information. As my father explained this situation, he said he was like a cigarette, one side was burning while the other side was bitten and locked between the lips. It was what we would call a Catch-22. He knew that someone in the area had reported that he was seen giving the Rhodesian forces directions of where to find the freedom fighters.

Soon after, my father was taken by the Vanavevhu and warned that he should not be talking to the Rhodesian forces. It so happened that the freedom fighters had encountered an awfully bad battle where one of them was killed. They had come under heavy gunfire from an ambush in a different area as they crossed the Runde River.

It was apparent that my father's life was in danger. Both sides, the Rhodesian soldiers and the freedom fighters, wanted him for questioning. Selling out the freedom fighters would lead to him being beaten up and possibly to death or permanent injury. The Rhodesian forces were also notorious for snatching people at night and torturing them. Some would be released afterwards but many never made it back home.

Around this time, one of my cousins who recently died was caught after a nasty battle that lasted several hours during the night. It was in a remote area and I remember that to visit our uncle my dad used to park his car ten kilometres away and then go the rest of the way by foot. The place was a flat area crossed by many small streams carved out by the swift rainwater flowing from the mountains. The soil in that area is a mixture of sand and silt, which made it hard for any roads to be made permanent as every year small deep streams destroyed the roads.

Because of this, the Vanavevhu had taken over the area. They knew the Rhodesian fighters could not reach it using their Crocodile-type trucks. But the Rhodesian forces one time decided to surround the area and drive the freedom fighters out. The Vanavevhu had set up a way to monitor any movement into the area. Young men of all ages were told if they saw the Rhodesian forces, they needed to report it to their parents and the parents would somehow get word to the freedom fighters. Even if you were ten you had to do this. If you were a boy over the age of sixteen you would qualify to carry messages to the freedom fighters about where the Rhodesian forces had been seen and what direction they were going in.

That information put the freedom fighters on high alert and their default reaction was to walk to higher ground, where they would use binoculars to monitor the plains below and watch the Rhodesian forces. The Rhodesian forces had walkie-talkies and an elaborate military radio system. The freedom fighters did not have any radios for communication, so they used messengers. But the Rhodesian forces had figured out that this was how the messages were moved. Hence if you were a boy of that age, you were more likely to be stopped and captured by the army. Sometimes it was just for the day and you'd be released in the morning after torture and questioning about the whereabouts of the freedom fighters. If you ran away, you could get shot.

My brother Martin had his first encounter with the Vanavevhu while he was in high school. He came back home from his boarding school for holidays and that night he got called to the base for a pungwe session. This was an all-night event with the freedom fighters, where there was singing and being told about the reasons for fighting the war. Young men his age in school were the prime target for the freedom fighters. They needed to enrol more of them, or to at least have an enthusiastic group of young men ready to join and fight. Some did drop out of school to join the war. My brother decided to stay in school.

Martin later told me that he had considered joining the Vanavevhu as he saw the injustice the Indigenous people of Zimbabwe, the Black people, were facing and at that point it all made sense. However, my brother had one problem. He grew up not very athletic; he is more of a thinker. He told me he knew that he could not survive the harsh conditions of the forest. Instead, he concentrated on his schooling and he explained that he hoped to do well in school and go into law so he could help his people. My brother achieved his dream of being a lawyer. That was how he would contribute, but he positively knew that if he tried joining the fighting he would die in the bushes.

There were many young men his age who did run away to join the freedom fighters; it sounded cool at that age. Some never came back and some came back with post-traumatic stress disorder, which was never diagnosed. A few came back and continued with their lives, taking advantage of the programs set up for ex-combatants. War has many results. The general idea can be achieved while individual experiences remain varied and complicated. From loss of life, loss of limbs or not ever being found to the joyous excitement of liberation. Freedom is complicated.

One day the Vanavevhu came to Martin's boarding school and told the principal to call all the students in for a meeting in the hall. They told the students that they needed more support to fight the Rhodesian forces. They told the students that they wanted to take everyone to a training camp in Mozambique. However, it was not time yet. It was a pungwe session at the school. By the end of it my brother told me a lot of students were ready to join them.

When the freedom fighters left, they asked the principal not to report to the police until after three days. However, the principal reported the incident the next day. The principal was surprised when he heard that the Rhodesian forces already knew what was going on and that they did not want to attack the freedom fighters on that day, because they did not want students to be killed.

My sisters had different problems during the war. After the war was in full swing, my sister Nicky had come back from boarding school in Dadaya. She was in high school, at the age where she was supposed to be cooking and delivering food to the freedom fighters. Girls doing this work were known as "Vanachihwido."

The day after she came back from school, word came in that the freedom fighters were in the area. Nicky was asked to go to a house where they were collecting the contributions from all the locals for cooking. They cooked the food and the girls were sent out, carrying food on their heads, pretending it was buckets of water.

Once the girls arrived at the base, they delivered the food and were asked to sit in a group while the freedom fighters ate. The girls had sat down for less than a minute when gunfire erupted. People scattered in all directions. My sister was inexperienced in the war, so she got lost in the bushes trying to run back home. She ended up in an open field.

Bullets were falling around her as she ran through the field. Someone called for her to get down. Eventually she got out of the field and ducked back into the bushes. One of the girls asked Nicky to follow her and told her not to go back home because the Rhodesian forces were going to go to people's homes looking for the freedom fighters. The two girls ran in the opposite direction of the village and crossed the Runde River to a place called Kwa-Bachi, about ten kilometres away. They ran most of the time. My sister had never been to these rural areas before, but they finally came to a village where they described what had happened. The villagers had heard the gunfire. It was common to help other villagers running away during the war. People knew that their turn to run away would come also if fighting broke out in their area.

For dinner my sister and the others were served sadza and some sort of salted and roasted insects called "mandera" in Shona. This insect is found in certain trees called msasa. Mostly poor families eat this insect either salted and dried or in a stew. The easy way is to dry it, add salt and to prepare it for dinner you would just need to add water and fry it. My sister refused to eat this; the host family tried to persuade her but she said she could not eat the insects. She went to bed with an empty stomach and pretended she was not hungry.

A family who said they were related to my father's second wife took them in; however, on that same day the Vanavevhu reached the village where my sister and the other people had fled. This was the same group that had been involved in the fight the day before and they demanded for people to come out to a base. They had a wounded freedom fighter there who needed help with his wounds and they wanted food. Whenever Vanavevhu came in with one of them wounded they were not very nice; they wanted people to respond fast. Most of the time they would stay in the bushes and get people to prepare food as quicky as possible, then leave, disappear into the forests.

My sister was terrified and refused to go to the base. She stayed in that home and told the family that she was sick. Most freedom fighters did not want to meet with sick people for fear of getting sick as well. So my sister faked being sick. However, if the Vanavevhu found out she was lying she could have been punished by being beaten with a stick in front of everyone. That was the freedom fighters' way of making sure they got the support they demanded. The next day the freedom fighters disappeared into the forest.

My sister and her friend decided to go back home the day after the Vanavevhu left. My sister told me that they walked through the bushes following the narrow paths, listening for any noise. If they heard people talking, they would run from the path and into the bushes to hide till the people passed. During that time young girls were fearful of meeting strangers as they could be assaulted. Especially at their age they were vulnerable to being sexually abused. There were many stories of girls running away from strange people in the forest called "Mabinya" who were assaulting young girls. Although this was not a rampant issue, young girls were always told to be aware of their surroundings and run away from strange people.

By this time my parents feared that my sister had been captured by the Rhodesian forces and were asking other people if they had seen Nicky. Other girls who were used to the war had stayed in the bushes around the river, hiding in the thick vegetation, so they were already back home.

When my sister and her friend arrived home in the afternoon, my mother was sobbing. My parents decided at that time that my sister should not be there.

A week or so after that incident, my mom and dad decided to send my two sisters, Nicky and Evelyn, to my aunt in Mashaba, a small mining town. My sister Evelyn was much younger; she was about thirteen and was also at risk. The day was set but as my mother prepared for them to leave, the Rhodesian forces arrived in the area on foot. They were spotted by one of the villagers near the river and then they decided to camp right next to the school. Normally the soldiers would not do anything to anyone if there was no fighting and so they sat under the trees next to the school eating their food.

The plan was for my sisters to walk to a place called Mabasa and then take the bus to Zvishavane, then catch another bus to

Mashaba. My mom decided to give my sisters bags of cornmeal and have them pretend to be going to the grinding mill, which was ten kilometres away. This was normal. Girls were known to carry these jute bags on their heads to go to the grinding mill. When the soldiers and the freedom fighters would stop the girls to ask them where they were going, they would let them go once they found out that they were going to the grinding mill. So my mom sent my sisters out past the camped soldiers with the jute bags of dried corn. The Rhodesian forces saw them, greeted them and left them alone.

My sisters had walked for about an hour – half the journey – when they heard the unmistakable sound of the Rhodesian forces' trucks coming from the direction in which they were going. They ran into the bush towards the next village. From the village they saw the empty trucks pass by on the road. Scared to keep going, they stayed in the village for a couple of hours before continuing. They were told by the villagers not to use the main road anymore and so they continued via winding paths around streams and hills.

My mom's plan was once they reached Mabasa, the girls would dump the bags and catch a bus to Zvishavane, and then from there make their way to Mashaba. My sister told me that as soon as they could see the bus stop from a distance they threw the bags down on the side of the road and ran as fast as they could to the bus stop.

They got to the Mabasa bus stop just as the bus was rolling into the station. My mom told them not to ever come back home, though eventually they did.

The trucks that my sisters saw were coming to pick up the

Rhodesian forces that were camped at the school. The Rhodesian forces had developed tactics for picking up soldiers and it was their way to never to use the same road twice. This was done to keep from being ambushed by the freedom fighters on their way back, which had happened in some areas. The freedom fighters would watch the Rhodesian forces from the mountains and if they saw the trucks were empty, they would know that they were going to pick up a group of soldiers. Then the Vanavevhu would wait for the truck to come back full of soldiers and ambush it.

The Rhodesian forces had watched the area around Chamini for a while and now they planned to drive the freedom fighters out. They planned one of their biggest attacks yet. They had helicopters, Crocodile trucks, spotting planes and bomb-dropping planes. I remember hearing the loud thuds from the bombs and hearing gunfire all night.

There is something about the sound of gunfire, no matter how far it is: if you hear it, you will not sleep. It started around 10:00 p.m. – the rapid, unmistakable sound of the Rhodesian forces' machine guns. I still know the difference between the freedom fighters' machine gun sound and the Rhodesian forces' machine gun sound. These sounds still have not vanished from my head. The heavy machine gun fire was followed by the unmistakable sound of rapid fire, which is the faster and louder sound of the AK-47, the main weapon used by the freedom fighters. I remember the curvy bullet magazine of the AK-47, which was never carried by the Rhodesian forces.

Occasionally during these battles you could hear a big thud from a bazooka. I honestly did not know then the actual difference between bazookas and RPGs – to me they looked the same and the sound of the thud was so loud it was hard to distinguish. Both the Rhodesian forces and the freedom fighters carried this kind of weapon, so you could never distinguish from the sound which side fired the rocket. To me the gunfire sounded like the choreography of a morbid dance where you almost envision the response from both sides. In some cases, as you listened to the gunfire you could hear who fired last and you could almost predict the outcome of the battle just from the sound of the gunfire. Sometimes you could determine which direction the battle was moving in by the volume of the sound of the gunfire. If the sound was getting louder, it meant that the battle was coming towards you and that meant it was time for the family to grab what they could and run.

On this day, though, the battle broke out in a valley between two mountains by the Runde River and the sound was everywhere. You could not decipher which direction the war was going, as it was multiplied by echoes as the sound bounced off the mountains and was magnified by the valley. You could not distinguish between an echo or gunshot.

We could see the helicopters circling around. Once they were in the valley, they would go low and then rise up as if following the mountain profile. As the chopper manoeuvred higher into the air, you could hear the gunfire reverberating as the gunner in the chopper aimed at the mountainside where the freedom fighters would normally camp. The chopper dove and wove around in random patterns to avoid being shot down. After several bursts of gunfire from the helicopter, we watched as it flew low along the mountainside as if going for another pass. As the chopper began firing again as it moved to a higher position, I saw it become a ball of fire. I saw the fire in the air before I heard the sound. The sound followed a few seconds later and it was deafening. The chopper was shot down. I heard the RPG-7, then the helicopter explosion, then the echo of the RPG-7 again and then the explosion of the helicopter again. The night sky lit up as if there were floodlights as different balls of fire rapidly moved towards the ground. These were secondary explosions from the falling wreckage. The silence that followed was deafening. It was almost as if we were watching Fourth of July fireworks. That finale when you see and hear the last boom and the silence that follows.

This situation was not good for us and all the other local villagers in the area. In that silence after the helicopter went down, you could feel the disturbance in nature. The normal night noise was disrupted and you could feel an eeriness in the night, a sense of danger, of fear, and the only answer was to run and run far away from this as possible. We had seconds to move and start running.

Everyone knew in the rural areas that whenever a helicopter was shot down the locals, if captured, would be questioned by the Rhodesian forces, be beaten and even tortured and then released with everlasting scarred memories. The Vanavevhu would disappear for days from an area after a serious battle like this one. But they would always come back after a while. They would sneak back into the area and talk to their trusted contacts who remained secret to most people. These contacts were responsible for telling the freedom fighters who sold out. In some cases, the contacts gave incorrect information as they tried to look as if they knew more than they did. That information could lead to people being punished by the freedom fighters without having done anything. In some cases they would be killed.

We had been hiding in the bush away from the house because many people had been burnt in their houses during these battles, so it was safer not to stay inside. Normally we would hide near the cattle kraal. My father always said it was better to be outside and that the cattle helped to mask our sounds when needed. Also, if there was moonlight, he would release the cattle and their movements would cause cowbells to ring and muffle the noise from our footsteps. This would help us to run away undetected. As we went past the cattle kraal that night, we opened the gate for the cows to get out.

After the helicopter went down my father took my eldest brother and disappeared into town. They travelled at night to Bulawayo. In Bulawayo they stayed with a cousin of my father. Although crammed in a tiny two-bedroom apartment, his cousin-brother and family were happy to see him. Some people slept on the living room floor. My father was given the kids' bedroom and the kids slept in the living room and sometimes the kitchen if the older people wanted to stay up late talking.

My mother, myself and four of my siblings – Paul, Sydney, Wilmore and Tomson – were left behind. The situation became more and more dangerous. The war was growing more intense by the day. The sound of guns was heard once or twice a week, with the firefights lasting from ten minutes to an hour. I saw bullets fall from the sky like red raindrops from passing helicopters. On a Friday afternoon at about midday, when school was almost over and the school kids were carrying out their chores, a battle broke out. This was a time when the whole school would clean the grounds together and some kids would be tasked with watering all flower beds. To water the flowers, the students would bring the water from a river half a kilometre way. The students would go in groups according to their grade.

It was during this time that the fight erupted and we got caught in the gunfire. My group was a few hundred metres away from the schoolyard when the gunshots started. There was pandemonium. I dropped the bucket of water that I was carrying and ran towards the water tank that was positioned under the fig tree. For a few minutes I stayed low with some other school kids and then there was a pause in the shooting. At this time people started running. I began running too. I could hear bullets penetrating the ground around me. At that moment I could not feel my legs. I did not know how fast I was running but I just kept going down the narrow path leading to the river as fast as I humanly could.

I saw other students and teachers running in front of me; no one looked back and no one stopped. It was a matter of running fast and going as far as possible from the rain of bullets. I saw some teachers help a student who been hit in the thigh by a bullet. They carried him using the double-human-crutch method, where the arms of the injured person are supported by the two people's necks and shoulders as the injured person is dragged along in the middle, as blood formed a trail behind him. I could hear him sobbing as I ran past them. I ran until I reached the riverbank. When I got there, most students had already reached the river and were crossing to safety. Once on the other side of the river, the gunfire subsided and we began to walk into people's homes.

The homes were right on the banks of the river, so finding safety was almost on a first-come, first-served basis. Some homes would tell you as you approached that they had enough people, but once you were taken in you would pretend to be a member of the family. The hunt for a place to sleep went on till I found some people who knew my parents. People were very generous in opening up their homes to the students.

The next morning, I started asking other people if they had seen my parents. I heard that my mom was seen crossing the river with another group. They went past the home we were staying in since it was already full. I waited until they came through the village on their way back and by then my mother had already been told where I was.

The local men had gone up the mountains to watch from the high point to see if the village would be destroyed or not. Normally the men would follow the family if the village was destroyed and tell people not to come back early. Parents would move around looking for their kids if they split up, or some kids would join other fleeing groups. In these communities, people knew each other so well that you would quickly find your family. My mother found me and said thank you to the family who kept me for the night. My mom and I started walking back home slowly. She seemed tired. She had spent the whole morning looking for me, going from village to village.

During the war I learnt to sleep in such a way that if any sound outside occurred, I would wake up immediately. For years I have boasted of this power. My wife and kids are amazed and they cannot figure it out. It also has its downside, as sleeping is always a problem for me. I lie in bed and I start summarizing the day, from morning to sunset, and I also plan for the morning. For this reason, it takes me a long time to sleep. As a child I used to be awake in bed for long hours thinking I was protecting my family and that I would run to my mum's room and wake her up and help her gather food for a couple of days or so if we needed to. There is a sound made by the Crocodile troop carriers, the trucks used by the Rhodesian forces, that I will never forget. In the quiet night of our rural area you could hear these trucks five kilometres away.

That unmistakable sound just got you awake and ready to run. The roar of the diesel truck mixed with the chattering of the loose gravel hitting the mudguards of a heavy metal body and the unmistakable growling sound of the engine as the heavy army truck went up and down the dirt road. By now almost everyone in our village knew the sound of the Rhodesian army trucks and the type of gun being fired. We could judge from the sounds, from the time it took for the gun sounds to stop and how far away they sounded, how rapidly gun exchanges happened. Based on this they could decide whether they should start fleeing to the mountains or to other villages.

The morning after running away, if you were split from your family, you would start looking for them, walking door to door, village to village, to locate your family, as my mother had done for me. Normally it would not take much time; everyone knew everyone so after the first couple of villages someone would point you in the right direction.

As the war continued and it got even worse my mom was also getting more worried about our survival.

CHAPTER 2
ESCAPE TO MASHABA

After my father and eldest brother had left for Bulawayo and my other brother Martin and sister Nicky had left for secondary school, my sister Evelyn (the one I come after) and the rest of my young brothers – Paul, Sydney, Wilmore and Tomson – and my mother remained at home at Chamini. Our house was behind the store, in fact the door from my mother's bedroom lead straight into the store. My father had built it so that after you close the store you would not have to carry the money out of the store but could just walk straight into the house.

The freedom fighters were still getting food from my father's shop without paying for the goods. When the local people would come to look for flour to make bread and basic ingredients such as salt and sugar, they would sometimes bring a list from the freedom fighters as well. The lists were comprised, most of the time, of cigarettes, canned corned beef and Coca-Cola drinks in cases of twenty-four 300-millilitre bottles. We later found out that sometimes the locals who were sent would change the numbers so they could get an extra pack of cigarettes or drinks. Normally my mother was the one responsible for running the store, while my father was responsible for going to Zvishavane and sometimes Gweru to order the goods for the store. When my father went away it was very difficult to get goods for the store and my mum would have to catch a bus to Zvishavane to order a few things such as bread, salt and sugar. But as the war went on the store was mostly empty. Some days it was not even necessary to open the doors; people were not coming to the store.

My mother instead focused on the vegetable garden that was situated close to the river. In the garden my mother planted green vegetables, tomatoes and onions. We would go to the garden towards the end of the day to water it, as well as take a bath. We would also bring back water from the river in containers for drinking and cooking. There is a way to filter the water from the river that, to this day, is still being used by rural people. First, you find a sandy patch near the river – I would describe it as a sandy beach – about a metre or so away from the running water and you dig a hole in the sand. The water from the river starts seeping into the hole, which filters the water. It works perfectly. Even if the water in the river looks slightly discoloured, when you use this method, the water flowing through the sand comes out looking clean. The hole in the sand is called "Tsime." The good thing is when you are done extracting your water you just push the sand back into the hole.

Vanavevhu would stay in the thick woods during the day and at night they would call the people to their base. The locals would cook them meat and vegetables and make tea. In some cases, they would ask if someone had a home-brewed batch of alcohol and would demand beer. Sometimes at night the freedom fighters would send the young girls to my father's shop, where they asked for cooking ingredients such as flour, cornmeal, bread, salt and sugar, as well as soft drinks and sweets. My mother always knew what they wanted.

The flour was used to cook breakfast for the freedom fighters, who would stay more than one night if there was someone injured in the group. The most common breakfast was something called "fat cakes" and rich creamy tea made from Tanganda tea, a local favourite, and fresh milk, often from a cow that was milked by hand by the local cook. The fat cakes are essentially self-rising flour, eggs, salt and, in some cases, sugar. This a very easy recipe similar to making pancakes but instead of cooking them in a pan you drop morsel-sized balls into a pot and deep-fry them. The self-raising flour and eggs in the balls make them double in size once cooked, turning them into fat, fluffy balls. I must admit when properly cooked they are really good. This is still a favourite breakfast component for families in the rural areas who can afford to buy flour.

My parents in most cases gave in to the requests from the Vanavevhu out of fear of being beaten at the base by the freedom fighters. One time my mother said no and the kids went running back to the freedom fighters to report that my mom had refused to give them flour and cooking oil. She was called to a house just at the edge of the hill where the freedom fighters had assembled. She was sat down and threatened that she would be beaten for refusing to supply them with grocery items. At that point my mom was very scared; she knew that if they continued giving out food with no payment, they would soon be unable to replenish the stock in the store. My family depended on the store's small profits for our future. They would send the rest of the children to boarding school like my older brothers and sister.

Some shop owners in other rural areas were not as lucky as my mother. For them, there was no warning. They got a flogging and in some cases were killed for refusing to supply the freedom fighters with food. Early on my father was told that he was expected to order more food and that the food should not run out. But the more he ordered, the more they came from kilometres away, as people knew that my father's store had goods. Freedom fighters spread the news to go to Chamini – there is a businessman who is supplying food. What the Vanavevhu did not know was that my father was now taking money from his savings and that the money was running out. Eventually there was going to be nothing in the store.

My father talked about what would happen when the money ran out and there were no more goods in the store. He knew the freedom fighters would kill him. They would kill him because they would think that he was refusing to support them.

It was becoming increasingly difficult to get money to buy goods for the shop. In a few months there would be nothing left to sell. There was no reason to have the shop doors open. My mom and dad were faced with this huge problem for they saw what they had worked for so hard just disappearing in the name of liberation struggle. For my parents this was not liberation but sinking into poverty. After my father left the store was closed most of the time.

The store and the house behind it were located next to the main road and because of the location we were a target. My father always told us that the reason for building the store at this location was twofold. First, it was in a central location in this rural area, so my siblings and I would not have to walk far to school and because the school was a central point in the village, most people would visit and buy stuff from the shop. Also, since he owned a car, he wanted to have the store and our home next to the main road.

My father used to tell us that the school was the most important part of choosing the location. He wanted his kids to be close to the school to have easy access to education. I remember he used to talk to my teacher after school to hear how his children were performing. The area where we grew up was remote and there was really no entertainment, therefore after school some teachers came to the shop to just talk to my father. They would talk in English and many teachers liked to talk to my father – they considered him to be wise. My father read the newspapers, even if they were past news. During my father's trips to town he would pick up a bunch of newspapers and he would read them whenever he was able to, relaxing, sitting under a big old tree in front of the store. Some teachers would come over and sit with him and they would talk about what was going on with the war, which had seemed so distant before it arrived in Chamini. The teachers often asked my father for a ride to town on Fridays to go and buy clothes and school supplies.

For all the good reasons my father had built the store where he had, during the war it became a problem. Our home could be seen from any of the mountains; it attracted attention. Everyone stopped there. Eventually we moved out of the house behind the store and into a mud-and-pole shed to get way from being a target.

When the war was at its climax some teachers ran away. The school was only partially open and students were regularly absent as well. Sometimes it was not necessary for the teacher to take a roll call as only half the class would be present, especially for the grade sevens who were thirteen to fourteen years of age.

These were the young kids who often became "Mujiba," which was the term for boys who were sent out to gather information on the places the Rhodesian fighters were. These young boys would then carry this information in letters hidden in their school bags. Now I have to explain about a school bag. These are not what you might think. Mostly school bags were used plastic ten-kilogram mealie-meal bags. Some kids had their parents make bags out of leftover jute grain bags, but I have to admit the best of them all was a special bag called "Nhava." This was a bag made out of the bark of a tree. The process is to peel the bark from a tree and then chew the bark in your mouth to soften the thick skin below the bark called "Gonzi." The bark of the tree tastes sour and there is a belief that the juice from the tree's bark helps kill harmful bacteria in the mouth, as well as strengthen and clean your teeth. I think there is some truth to it, for as you chew the fibre that action cleans your teeth. After you chew the bark, it becomes a nice and soft fibre. You then wash the fibre in water and sun-dry it. You could also do it by handwashing the fibre, but I tell you the chewed stuff is much better.

So every day, as you went out herding the cattle, you would find this specific type of tree and peel off a strip of bark, chew it and store the materials. When you started making the bag you gathered the dried material and dipped it in water first, then you carefully wove three strands of fibre at a time, crossing them one over the other. It's actually a very relaxing motion – I can compare it to playing with one of those fidget spinners. The only difference is that you end up with a nice handmade bag. Weaving bags was once part of the educational curriculum called arts and crafts and by the time I got to grade seven I had a self-made school bag of my own.

The hut we moved into was about three-quarters of a kilometre away, in what is called a "Maraini." Maraini literally means "lines," but today the term is used by the young people to just mean a neighbourhood. These are clusters of huts and houses built in lines alongside hills, mountains, roads and rivers. A family's group of huts would be bedrooms and a kitchen. The kitchen was the main gathering area for the family; this is where you would find the family sitting around at night talking and waiting for the food to be ready. Normally in the centre of the hut would be the fire where the mother would cook, with the girls helping the mother. Our hut was built very quickly by one of the villagers who was friends with our family. We did not have a kitchen, so all the cooking was done outside. The hut was our only hut and mainly for sleeping. I remember the door was a thin, galvanized corrugated metal roofing sheet that was taken from the store's veranda. There were holes on the door from the nails that were used to secure it on the metal sheet on the roof. We used to peep through those holes if we heard footsteps outside. We slept on the floor, and with your head directly on the floor you could hear all sorts of footsteps – from moving cattle to people walking along the path close by to the unmistakable sound of soldiers' or freedom fighters' footsteps.

I remember one night a group of soldiers passed by the narrow path right in front of our hut. In the dead of night, you could hear it so loudly. The moon was high up the sky and so bright it was as if it was daylight. I could see them through the hole in the door as they walked past, one after another in a straight line. I could not see what they were wearing but could make out their guns swinging on their shoulders. The movement in a straight line was the tell that they were Rhodesian forces. The freedom fighters never moved in a straight line, they moved a little faster and more chaotically. Sometimes they moved in two split groups. You would see five people and then you see another five a minute or two after.

The hut needed to store all our food and clothes and have place for sleeping. All the cooking was done outside. My mother had no choice but to cook all the food earlier than she normally would, before sunset, because at night the cooking fire could be seen from afar, which would attract the soldiers. Basically, no one cooked outside at night during the war for fear of being a target.

It was crowded in the hut with clothes and blankets in one corner and a bag of cornmeal, some pots and dried meat in another. Dried meat was very common at the time because there was no refrigeration. People had to salt and dry the meat to keep it for long periods. I tell you, this meat is also tasty! It can be eaten as a snack or cooked. Essentially this is the biltong that you buy in shops these days. My favourite dish was when the dried meat was mixed with handmade peanut butter, fresh tomatoes and vegetables and boiled for a long time, till the dried meat was soft again. The peanut butter stuck to the bottom of the pot and formed a crust – that crust was so delicious. I would wait for my mother to finish cooking and dish the food and then she would let us have the pot. I would scrape the bottom of the pot with a wooden spoon and eat the crust. We ate the stew with sadza. First, you made a morsel – that is, you moulded a round lump of sadza to fit in the inside of your hand – and then you would dip it into the peanut butter dried-meat goulash.

We lived in the hut for about six to eight months. It was like an eternity for me. By this time the war was in full swing and going to school was sporadic. Often when fighting between the Rhodesian army and the freedom fighters occurred close to our rural area, school would be closed for days until the headmaster sent out word to the locals to let their kids come back to school. Sometimes the teachers would also run away to people's homes, but in most cases the Rhodesian forces did not bother teachers that much. Even the freedom fighters left teachers alone. The freedom fighters needed the schools to be open as they needed people to move around so they could move information around.

The government did not want to be seen as monsters depriving kids of education. However, with regular outbreaks of fighting schooling was definitely affected. No kid or teacher would sit in class knowing their lives would be in danger due to crossfire at any time.

Generally, if fighting occurred within an hour from an area by foot, the people living there would run in the opposite direction, heading to where the war was not being fought. This was because if either side of the fighting parties had any fatalities or causalities, they would come back and harass and kill people in areas close by in revenge.

Additionally, Rhodesian soldiers would drive to the closest rural area, claiming they were looking for the freedom fighters. In their pursuit of the fighters, they would ask people if they had seen any. If you said, "No," you could get a beating or you could be asked to come with them. The soldiers often made locals stand up in the back of a truck as they drove through the rural areas. This was a clever trick by the Rhodesian forces. They knew that the freedom fighters never attacked them with civilians in the truck. Sometimes they would take a local without even questioning or beating them up and drive with them, always making sure the local could be seen. They would move from one rural area to another and then release the person far away and tell them to go back home by foot.

The act of using locals as shields was quite dangerous for people. If no one saw the local villager being picked up, then they saw you in the army truck, they might think that you were one of the Rhodesian forces' informants and therefore you were a sellout. If you were reported to the freedom fighters as a sellout, the punishment was to be beaten to death and then to be buried somewhere in the bush in a shallow grave. The beating was done in front of villagers at night and the local people were encouraged to participate. Young men who were aspiring to be freedom fighters were asked to do most of the beating. The whole thing was used to serve as an example to anyone who was thinking about betraying the freedom fighters. Some people got killed just like that, because someone reported them as being a sellout without real proof.

My family was a prime target because of the shop. Any shop or school in a rural area was a centre for the community. These places were where locals gathered for meetings and after church. After church on most holidays, especially during Christmas holiday week, people would come to the shop to hang out and meet their friends. Young men would meet up with their girlfriends, buy some Fanta or Coke and sugar buns, candy and biscuits. Sometimes my father played a record player in the shop and the young men and girls would be dancing right in front of the shop. Strangely enough my father did not want me and my siblings to dance with the crowd. He always asked us to stay vigilant and not lose ourselves in the dancing, as people would take advantage and steal from the store. The best we could do was to watch.

When anyone visited Chamini, they would pass by our home, because back then it was the only shop in the area. You'd walk for several kilometres before you could reach another store. My parents knew most people in the area by name, and often there was some kind of inferred relationship, such as calling visitors uncle or niece, as a sign of respect. The way it works in the Shona culture is that you always look for some kind of relationship with someone. When you meet someone, you ask for their last name and the big question you ask is for their "Mutupo." Usually that turns out to be an animal such as "Shumba," which refers to a lion; or "Mbizi," which refers to a zebra; or "Zhou," which refers to an elephant; or part of the body such as "Moyo," which means the heart. I grew up being told that Mutupo is a totem; I now know that totem is used in other parts of world as well, with a little different meaning. Using the totem, one tries hard to find a link to their and your mother's totem or your father's totem. It could even be a grandmother or grandfather with the same totem. If their totem is similar to your mother's or father's, you refer to them as your cousin. If you could not find any totem linkage, you would refer to them as "Baba," which means father, or "Mukoma" or "Sisi," which means brother or sister. It is a bit complicated, but the Shona people always try and find a relationship with someone so that they can respectfully address you. Even the freedom fighters used to ask people what their totem was to try and make themselves closer to the people by addressing themselves as if they were related to the locals.

The soldiers from both sides also found that the shop was a place they could get supplies such canned foods, drinks and, for the freedom fighters, even clothes. One thing I found out is that when someone is carrying a gun, even if it is not pointed at you, when they ask you for a drink or something you just give them it without asking for money.

I still remember the day we finally abandoned our hut and

home and left for Mashaba. It was after my father and big brother had sneaked back home one Sunday to come and see the family. He hugged all of us when he came back from hiding for that day. It was a tense moment. People had warned us that the Rhodesian forces were on top of the mountain watching our home and the store to see if my father came back and to watch for the freedom fighters to come back as well, possibly looking for food and cigarettes. Also, some unidentified men had been spotted along the river posing as freedom fighters and saying they were looking for directions to the local shop, my home.

My father left just as the sun set. If he had not left that night, he would have been killed. Sure enough, that same night around midnight, there was a loud knock at the door. At first my mom kept quiet, but the knock grew louder. It was more pounding at the door than knocking. Someone called out my father's name. "Makonese, open up!" they said in Shona, the local language, and demanded for the door to be opened immediately.

My mother answered and asked them to identify themselves, which was the normal procedure with the so-called Comrades or freedom fighters. The voice replied that they were the Comrades and that they wanted to talk to my father about something important. My mother answered that my father had been there that afternoon but had left for town. Now the man's voice suddenly sounded irritated and forceful. He demanded that everyone inside the house come out or they would burn the house with everybody in it. My mother told us to get up and follow her as she held the candle in her hand. We all came out and were made to line up away from the door, facing a couple of men who were clad in what looked like jeans. They almost looked like the freedom fighters, but they stood in a formal way, which the freedom fighters never did.

As we got out of the house, I noticed that there were several men with their guns pointed at the doorway, ready to shoot. Freedom fighters never stood in one place, they always moved with no proper stance or order or fashion. I was confused and scared. I could now see several other figures in the dark, some lying down with their guns pointed towards the door. My mom held the candle in her hand as we stood in line. The man shouted again my father's name as he entered the house carrying a huge flashlight. Two men quickly went into the house, turning beds upside down and kicking chairs and shouting, "Makonese, come out now!" The two men came out with their flashlights, shouting to my mother, "Where is he hiding?"

My mother replied in a shivering voice, "I told you he left earlier today; he was scared the Rhodesian soldiers would kill him. He does not know the freedom fighters' whereabouts." The man asked her why would they kill him? My mother answered because they think that he was supporting the Comrades with food and that he knew where they were.

The man answered, "You mean terrorists?" One of the men who was carrying a bright flashlight pointed both the light and his gun into our faces. The combination of shining light in my eyes and a gun barrel was intense. The gun barrel was so close that I could smell the metal and gun oil. It was a strange smell. I had never been so close to a gun before. I had seen guns; however, to have a gun barrel in your face is different. It seems much bigger when it is that close to your face. The dark hole behind the shining light on my face was too much for me. I could not feel my legs. I was scared and confused. The light was so bright; the oily scent from the tip of the gun was so strong. Several thoughts ran through my head as I looked at the man behind the flashlight. Such as how in a matter of minutes we would all be dead. There were whispers from the dark and I could sense there were many more soldiers in the bush. The whole scene was unlike the freedom fighters – the huge flashlights, the clothing and orderly behaviour. Even the way they carried their guns was not like the freedom fighters.

As the dark shadows gathered and whispered to each other, they made a promise to my mother that they would come back for my father. The man shut off the light and I was in a state of temporary blindness. The commander gave orders to start moving. We were left standing there and within a minute or so the soldiers disappeared into the night. I could barely see now from the small candle that my mother still held. The wax had covered her hand. You could hear the footsteps fade away as they moved quietly into the night. My mum lead us back into the house. She did not put the candle out; she just sat on the edge of the bed as she told us to go to sleep. I got into a sleeping position, but was wide awake, listening. I could hear my mum praying in a whisper. After several minutes, the night fell silent again.

My mom had asked everyone to go to sleep, but we never slept. Everyone lay there quietly but fully awake. It was clear to all of us what had happened. These were the Selous Scouts, the special forces wing of the Rhodesian army who posed as freedom fighters. They had come to try and take my father away to either kill or torture him.

When the soldiers left our home, they went across to the school headmaster's house and they took him with them. They knew that the headmaster was friends with my father and that he possibly knew where my father was hiding. They took the headmaster to a location in the woods close to the mountains where they questioned him about my father – whether he knew where my father was staying or if my father had told him when he was coming back.

The headmaster was tied up in a style called "mbira dzakondo." This is where you are made to sit on the ground and have your knees pointed up while your feet are flat on the ground. A stick is passed under your knees and your arms are made to go under the horizontal stick and tied with your arms pushing the stick up against the back of your knees. This renders you immobile and is uncomfortable for long periods of time. It is normally accompanied by sitting someone near a fire. Because you are tied up you cannot move away from the fire so the heat gradually burns you. You would feel like you are slowly getting roasted like a chicken. Sometimes they would drag someone closer to the fire, letting the heat literally cook them alive to force them to tell the truth or admit to guilt.

The headmaster told them that, yes, my dad had left earlier and promised them that if my father ever came back, he would send one of the school kids to walk all the way to their military camp to tell them. They pulled him away from the fire and left him tied up all night. At daybreak he was released and was given a message for my family that they would be back and next time everyone would be killed if they did not find my father.

Once released, the headmaster came over to our house. He told my mother what had happened. I had never seen the headmaster of the school looking like that. He was dirty and he did not have shoes on. He looked like a kid who had been playing and rolling in mud; his black skin was red from rolling on the ground, from the red earth in our area. He quickly gave the message to my mother and disappeared to his house. Before he left, he whispered to her that we should pack our bags and go as soon as possible.

Right at that moment my mother decided we would escape. This had to be properly planned, as we always felt like someone with binoculars was watching us from the mountains. The soldiers and freedom fighters both used the same technique of going up the mountains to watch people's movements down in the valley before they approached the village. My mother told us that we may be watched by the soldiers and that she needed to come up with a plan for us to leave unnoticed and that we should not tell anyone of the plan. If word went around, the freedom fighters would take my mum and beat her up, claiming she was trying to escape from feeding the Comrades. On the other hand, the Rhodesian forces would probably follow us in the hopes that we would lead them to where my father was and kill him.

My mother decided that we would leave before the sun came out. She knew that it would take two hours to walk to Muzvond-iwa, where we could get a bus to go to Zvishavane or Shurugwi, which was in the opposite direction we wanted to go, but the idea was to get away into a town setting as quickly as possible then take a bus to Mashaba. My mother always planned. I guess it comes from growing crops in a rural area where my parents had to plan when to plant their crop based on when the rain may come, looking at winds, the trees and the formation of clouds in the sky. She planned the journey so that by the time daylight appeared we would be in the valley on the other side of the mountains and by then we could move faster as well and reach the main tarred road, which is now the highway.

My home is about ten kilometres away from the bus station by a normal road, but we could not walk along the road for fear we would meet someone who would tell the freedom fighters or the Rhodesian forces. Instead, we went through the mountain pathways.

On the day of departure, after we had locked up everything at the store and had secured the door at the hut, my mother told only one person that we were leaving – a neighbour who my father trusted. She told him that sooner or later we could be killed and that it was time for us to leave. Mr. Msipa agreed. He had heard stories about the soldiers looking for my father and was worried. My mother asked him to take care of our cattle and to check on our property once in a while.

We left home at three o'clock in the morning in the darkness, moving quietly and not talking at all. My mother told us we needed to be quiet until we reached the other side of the mountains. We each carried a bag, while my mother carried my youngest brother on her back and carried a huge bag on her head. This was basically a sheet of cloth or blanket with all four corners tied together. We followed her in the dark for about two hours before dawn came. We headed for an opening between two mountains, a valley that led to the back of the mountain and which had a path used by cattle movers and hunters. We went up and down streams of water flowing from the mountains, up and down small rocky hills. This area is part of the great dike, a band of short, narrow ridges and hills that runs for 550 kilometres north to south across the country. There was no shortage of hills and while you get used to walking up and down in this environment, during the night it's a different ball game. About halfway there, my mum fell and landed on her knees. The bundle she was carrying on her head fell as well and tumbled a few feet down the side slope of the path. My youngest brother, Tomson, who was one year old, did not fall because by falling to her knees my mum had prevented him from slipping through the carrier. She did not cry out, but I knew she was in pain. I could hear her heavy breathing, but for fear of being heard she just silently moaned for a minute. We helped her up and picked up the bags. There was no time to check if she was hurt. She said she was fine and that we had to keeping moving. We kept on walking.

As dawn approached, we could see the path clearly and could see some animals start to move in the bushes. We were not talking, and it was so quiet you could only hear our footsteps. As the path started changing from rough, rocky ground to finer clay and sandy soil we knew we were in the area called Muzvondiwa.

The bus station on the major road was getting closer. We moved faster. In the area close to the station there was not much fighting so as we approached the highway station we all felt more free and we started talking a little. If you have ever gone hiking in thick forest, you know how winding natural paths can be, but if it's a matter of life or death and you're escaping from a war zone, you do not get tired, your feet do not hurt. It does not matter how steep the hills are. Even if you feel the pain, you ignore the pain. I remember I only felt how tired I was when we got to Zvishavane.

We arrived at the station very early and the first bus coming from Shurugwi to Zvishavane was going to be there around eight. There is no fixed time and so the bus can be there at eight or ten o'clock, so we waited for a few hours. The waiting felt like such a long time as we sat on our bags, looking at a long stretch of two-way tarmac road. At that time these roads were not busy; you would see a car pass by maybe every twenty minutes. The roads were especially quiet at night during the war.

Sitting at the side of the road you could hear the sound of the oncoming traffic echoing through the valley. You'd hear a bus or transport truck way before you'd see it. I do not know what type of engine was in the Rhodesian forces' trucks, but they had a distinct sound. We'd listen carefully to all the traffic sounds and once something was identified as a Rhodesian forces' truck, people would run into the Muzvondiwa village. It was dangerous to be found by the Rhodesian forces at the bus station. They would stop and find out who you were and where you were going. Sometimes the soldiers would tell you to go back to where you were coming from. For my family it would be extremely bad. I sat there quietly, listening for any sound, with my eyes fixed on the direction from which the bus would be coming.

I started hearing what sounded like a heavy truck. Everyone was quiet as they listened to the sound of the vehicle approaching around the bend. As it came up a slight incline, you could hear the heavy engine change gears. No one moved, until someone from the village called out, "It's the bus." Everyone was on their feet with their baggage in their hands and some on their heads. Finally, the bus arrived. My mum waved for it to stop. As the bus stopped, it hit the gravel and a plume of dust followed. The dust engulfed us as the bus conductor grabbed the bags and climbed up the back of the bus to the roof where he placed and tied them down. As soon as he was done tying the baggage, he whistled loudly to signal to the bus driver to start moving. All this happened very fast. The bus driver and the conductor had a rhythm and by the time we found seats at the back of the bus, the bus was already moving. The buses along the Muzvondiwa road started moving even as the conductor still hung on the door, one foot hanging out, hopping in as he slammed the bus door.

The conductors on these buses still do it to this day; it's like a dance. The loading of people and goods takes very little time and the driver does not wait for you to sit down. I am not sure how someone has not been hurt by now. But that day I looked out the windows as the bus started speeding down the road. As the bus took a curve in the road, I had a last glimpse of Muzvondiwa. There was a feeling of happiness and confusion. All I knew was we were heading away from the horror and I was certain that anything we would see in this war was not going to be as frightening as that gun barrel in my face. I was wrong.

We were headed to my aunt's place in Mashaba, where my

mother planned to leave me and my younger brother Paul. The bus arrived in Zvishavane around midday, after we had spent the whole morning travelling on the bus. The reason the bus took so long to get to Zvishavane is because it stopped at every bus stop and even at places that were not marked as bus stops to pick up anyone who waved for the bus. From Zvishavane we took another bus to Mashaba.

The bus was crowded, and naturally kids do not occupy a seat if there are elders with no seat. You always give your seat to those older than you to show respect. I remember feeling good that my mum was sitting in the seat as I stood next to her, holding onto the exposed metal curved above the bench seat. In these buses, which are often called chicken buses, luggage is all over and sometimes includes live animals such as small goats, but mostly chickens, hence the name "chicken bus." You could ask why chickens? Because during this time, and I am pretty sure it is still so today in some parts of the country, a live chicken was the gift of choice when visiting someone. The good thing about a live chicken is you can eat it for dinner, or you can keep it to produce eggs for you and you always remember who gave it to you. In some cases, one chicken multiplied from one gift to several chickens, which was life-changing for some families who now could enjoy the eggs and meat. This gift is similar to the way a guest in the Western world brings a bottle of wine when visiting.

We did not have a chicken to take to my auntie. There were no cellphones like these days and letters were not moving, so my auntie did not know we were coming. However, during this time it was not unusual for someone to just show up unannounced. In fact, in the Shona culture it is okay to just show up.

My aunt's house was very small, what was referred to as a matchbox house, a small mud-and-pole house that had two tiny rooms she called bedrooms. We could not all stay there. My aunt was already living with my grandmother, a worker who took care of my grandmother and my two sisters. My mum decided she was going to follow my father to Bulawayo. The township life was different from home, the cowbell sounds that I was used to hearing in the morning were replaced by the sounds of buses, cars and trucks. Even the smell was different, the nice clean air replaced by diesel and petrol fumes from motor vehicle exhaust.

My mum took my sisters and three of my younger brothers with her to Bulawayo, leaving me and my young brother Paul in Mashaba. My aunt had one bedroom and Paul and I and the worker used the other bedroom. There was one small bed that the worker could not sleep in because it was too small so Paul and I slept in the bed.

Mashaba is a mining town. The place was half rural area and half town, and the part of the town where my aunt lived was called the township, the area reserved for the Black citizens during those segregationist years. Township land belongs to the municipality and the job of the municipality is to provide people with piped water. During that time, before the independence, the residents would fetch water from a common place and bathe in common bathrooms, which were located in different central places all walking distance in the township. So if you needed to take a bath you either went to a common bath or you wheelbarrowed or carried some water in a plastic or metal container on your head to bathe in a large metal dish at home. Unlike the areas that were inhabited by the well-to-do, who were mostly white, where water was piped into the houses and were sparsely populated with nice backyards and well-groomed front yards.

My auntie was very loving, since she did not have kids of her own. She called us Georgie and Pauly as if we were her kids, and in fact in the Shona culture we are her kids, since we are her brother's kids. She told everyone around that we were her kids; everyone in the township knew us. My auntie had a small shop where she sold groceries to the miners who lived in the township. She also gave them on credit goods such as tea leaves, bread and milk. She would write their names and purchases down and the miners would pay at the end of the month when they got paid. This was the same method my father had used in an earlier store he had owned in the Zvishavane mine before the war started. My father would supply the miners with goods such mealie-meal and meat and record it in his notebook for payment on payday. People were very honest and would come back and pay my auntie on payday.

In Mashaba things were going well until just before dusk one day my brother and I saw at least five people wearing jeans and baseball caps leaving the township. Something in me told me that today was not a normal day. When we got back home, I told my aunt that we saw some suspicious men getting out of the town going towards the hills. My aunt, having lived in Mashaba for a long time, did not understand what I was talking about. She told me there were many people that came from outside of town to buy the goods in Mashaba, so I should not worry about it.

I thought about this as we walked back home from my aunt's shop. I said to her that I really felt like those were freedom fighters in the town and that we should lock our doors and make sure we were secure for the night. My aunt was a very nice person. She responded by reassuringly saying, "You know what, my son? I am going to follow exactly what you said and in order to make you feel happy we're actually going to put some chairs in front of the door and block the door. How do you feel about that?"

I replied, "That is great. I really feel something is wrong." My aunt had never seen the freedom fighters and she had never experienced the war. But I knew something was not right about those men.

We ate our dinner that night with my grandmother. I think she was almost one hundred years old at the time. She always made jokes because she couldn't see very far. In most cases she could not identify who she was looking at and relied on the sound of someone's voice to know them. My aunt said to her, "These boys are talking about some weird people that they saw this afternoon heading out of the town. We're going to be putting chairs in front of the doors and making sure that all the windows are closed. Grandma, if you hear anything, shout."

That night nothing happened and, in the morning, we just carried on with our normal lives. My brother and I went to school. After school we played soccer with other kids in the middle of the road. The same soccer balls that we had in Chamini were also popular here in Mashaba. However, softer and cleaner plastic bags were used to make them, since the boys had more access to discarded plastics in the rubbish bins in the township. The rubbish bins were only collected once a week and they were full, so after school that day all the boys went around to the rubbish bins collecting plastic bags for making soccer balls. We used pens that we picked up from the rubbish bins to write our names on the balls. I thought it looked very cool. Then we spent a long hour playing soccer in the middle of the road on the way back from school, just like we did every other day. This was a normal day for me and several other kids in the township.

The difference between Mashaba and our home area Chamini was that in Mashaba we did not have to go looking for cattle after playing soccer. You could either play soccer or go around people's yards stealing fresh fruits, such as mangoes and oranges. My auntie never wanted us to be involved with those naughty kids stealing fruits, so she was very happy to see us play soccer with other kids on the road. Sometimes she would stop by and cheer us on. There was more time in Mashaba for us to play and my aunt did not really mind. We made sure we did our chores – coming from the rural areas, we were very disciplined about helping at home. One of our chores was to keep the yard clean and we fed the chickens. My aunt's only other request was to tell her where we were at all times. She needed to know where we were playing and who we were playing with. Life was good in Mashaba, we felt like we had finally run away from the war for sure and forever.

However, in the back of my mind I still thought about the five men I saw going up the hill. With the experience I had in

Chamini, I suspected they were freedom fighters. From the stories I'd heard back home, I knew freedom fighters often left their guns in the bush and entered towns to go to regular shops. Most of the people from the township worked in the mine and had no idea what a freedom fighter looked like. They had never seen one. I knew that they were normal people who mostly looked like us, but I had seen how they walked and talked so I could spot them easily.

The image of when I first saw the freedom fighters stayed with me forever. I saw how they moved their eyes, how they almost covered each other's visual peripherals. I could not stop thinking about the people I had told my auntie about. I knew the freedom fighters were in town. Every now and then I would look up to the hills to see if there were people going up there or if there were people in the hills. I told my auntie that I knew something was going on. We started noticing more and more army patrols going on in the township. I knew it was just a matter of time before the war erupted. My auntie told a story one afternoon when a group of five people she could not identify came in the store and bought all the cigarettes and painkillers called Cafenol. She tried to have a conversation with them, but she could not get any information. I told her that we should be careful. She told us to stay close to home every day after school. For months nothing happened. It felt like everything was normal.

One night just after midnight I woke up to the sound of heavy footsteps and heavy breathing right outside our door. At that moment I felt like I was back in the war zone. All the fears and memories of the war and the things that happened during the war came flashing back through my brain. There were many footsteps that followed and they were the sound of heavy boots with the click of the metal straps that hold the boot together and the sound of the metal clips that hold the shoelaces of the military shoes together. We listened to the sound of heavy breathing we could clearly hear in the dead of night. I saw my aunt's shape as she crawled into our room. She threw herself to the floor and reached for our hands. She whispered for my brother and me to jump off the bed and get under it. But we were already under the bed. I knew who was outside the door. Within a second there were gunshots and flashing pieces of red metal hit the walls on the inside of the room. Glass shattered as the bullets pierced the windows. I had the same feeling I'd had during the war in Chamini. When I'm in such deep fear I tend not to feel my legs. It seems my brain is fully engaged and nothing else matters except survival. Have you ever heard about people who get hit by a bullet and don't realize that the bullet has pierced their flesh until they stop, then they realize they have been hit? Whether you call it adrenalin or shock, I can tell you it's real.

Lying on the floor under the bed is the safest way to avoid flying bullets but the downside is once you're on the ground the sounds get magnified tenfold. Every movement or sound coming from outside is translated via the ground directly into your body. You hear everything. I was lying down next to the wall, and I could hear and feel the bullets hitting the walls. Some pierced the thin walls and some bullets got embedded in the mud walls. I could hear a soldier moving quickly along the walls, seeking cover. I could hear the solider move away from the wall, his footsteps loud and clear. I heard the thud of someone falling, but did not know if they had been shot or were diving for cover.

My auntie's house was on the last row before you got out of the township to the hills. I could hear the echo of gunfire and I knew the freedom fighters were in the hills and the soldiers outside our house were the Rhodesian forces.

The brain is a funny thing. The amount of information it stores amazes me. At that moment I could decipher very clearly what kind of guns were being used. I knew it was the freedom fighters fighting the Rhodesian forces – I had heard all the sounds before. They sounded exactly the same as they had in Chamini.

This was the first time my auntie had heard fighting and she looked more scared than me and my brother. That moment was when I realized that sometimes having experience with something could get you around the block. The soldiers shouted vulgar things to each other, followed by the sound of grenades and more gunfire. We told her to lie still. I knew we had to hang on down there under the bed for as long as possible. The fighting would stop at some point. I heard the gunshots move from one direction to another. As the gunshots moved away from the house, I imagined in my head the direction that the soldiers were going. It was as if I could hear the gunshots going up the hill. Slowly the sound of battle faded and I could hear the screams from outside. I knew that the freedom fighters had left. They were used to quick firefights – I knew that they were all about saving the rounds of ammunition they carried. If the freedom fighters realized that there were too many Rhodesian forces in a battle, they would stop and vanish into the forest. As the gunfire faded to the hills, we kept lying there, not moving at all.

No one went back to bed. My aunt sat on the floor in the living room. Just before dawn, the silence was once again broken. The sound of heavy trucks approaching the township could be heard breaking through the silence of this horrid morning. We sat on the floor with my auntie as she whispered a prayer. We could hear the puff of the air brakes as the trucks stopped right in front of the houses in the last row before the hills.

It was almost daylight when the soldiers rushed out of the trucks. They moved to the back of the house where they picked up one dead soldier and threw him into the truck. You could hear the soldiers banging on doors and people screaming as they took a few dozen people for questioning. We were lucky no one came to our door. After a few minutes, the trucks moved to another part of the town. As that was happening, my auntie was already packing our bags. She did it without talking. I guess she was in shock.

After about three hours the trucks could be heard driving away from the township. We waited for another hour or so, as my aunt kept peeking through the corner of the curtains, until we heard the neighbours and other people come out. My auntie went out to talk to the neighbours and we followed her. In between the houses the neighbour was covering up with dirt the pool of blood that was left by the dead soldier. I realized that the big thud we heard was that falling soldier after he had been shot.

My auntie did not waste any time. The next day she put my brother and me on the bus and took us to Bulawayo. She left the housekeeper taking care of my grandmother.

It took four hours to get from Mashaba to Bulawayo. Once we got there, my auntie spent some time talking to my dad. The next day my aunt took a bus back to Mashaba. I had mixed emotions as she left. I knew she had to go and take care of my grandmother. I knew my grandmother could not be moved from the house; she could hardly walk anymore. She needed help to move from one point to another. Every day my grandmother would be helped outside to sit on her mat on the ground at the back of the house. Sometimes she asked to be moved into the sun and sometimes into the shade. The housekeeper was the person who was primarily responsible for helping my grandmother, but even she needed help. My aunt did not want her to quit so everyone was chipping in to help. So my aunt had to go back to Mashaba quickly.

After the war came to Mashaba, the security forces put a curfew in place. After 6:00 p.m. no one was allowed to be walking in the streets. There was a constant presence of Rhodesian forces protecting the asbestos mine and the mineworkers. The freedom fighters' whole reason for bringing the war to Mashaba was an attempt to scare the miners and cripple the mining, which would affect the government's finances.

Eventually the increase in protection from the soldiers brought some kind of normalcy to Mashaba and my auntie's shop was back in business. My grandma later passed away of just old age. Though there was no record of when she was born, some people say she was close to one hundred years old when she died. A few years after my grandmother died, my auntie also passed away of illness.

CHAPTER 3
THE HUNT FOR MY FATHER

When Paul and I got to Bulawayo my father was working for a company that paved roads. He was working as a driver, but the money he was getting was not enough for our big family, so my mother started selling tomatoes on a street corner. During the weekend, when we weren't in school, my brother and I also took to the streets with small bags of tomatoes and potatoes for sale. We walked in Mpopoma, the "high-density" or overcrowded and poor neighbourhood where we lived. We went from house to house, shouting, "Amatamatisi lapa!" and "Amagwili lapa!," which means "Tomatoes here!" and "Potatoes here!" Sometimes we would come across kids who went to the same school as us and we could see on their faces they felt sorry for us. In one or two cases, we were laughed at.

We prepared the tomatoes on Friday evenings. My mother

would buy small plastic bags that could fit four tomatoes for a dollar and she taught us that if a customer wanted to pay fifty cents, we could open the plastic bags and sell them half. I would carry four bags hanging from each hand, though as young boy that felt slightly heavy. My brother Paul would carry two per hand. Now you may be wondering how did we carry this? My mother had designed a carrying tool for us that was made of heavy-gauge wire. The carrying tool was an S-shaped figure turned upside down. Imagine that the centre part is your handle and the two open S sides facing up are the part you would push the knotted bag onto. There were two bags on each end of the S shape, with my hand in the middle.

Once I sold one bag of tomatoes, balancing became tricky and I had to quickly sell another bag to maintain the balance. Sometimes I would try and convince the customer to buy two bags of tomatoes to make it easier. Some customers just saw the awkwardness in balancing as soon as you removed one bag and offered to buy two. The quicker I sold, the faster it became lighter and it meant we could go home earlier. My mother told us that if we sold all the tomatoes, we could get a dollar to buy a cent cool, which was basically a plastic tube filled with coloured sweet juice. It was our favourite cheap drink.

On the streets life was a little different. I looked out for my little brother and he looked out for me as well. Some people would shout at us to shut up and get off their street. Some would be kind. I remember one lady who called us over as we passed by her home and offered us water, which we refused. My mother had told us not to eat food or drink water from people we did not know. So the lady asked us to wait at her gate for a moment; then she asked us where were from and if we went to school or not. We told her that we went to school during the week and during the weekend we helped our mother sell vegetables so we could get money to go to school and to eat. She then bought everything we had in our hands and even threw in a dollar extra for me and my brother. She told us she was very sad and that she was a teacher and we should not stop school. We should not give up. She also explained to us that she did not need all the vegetables but she was buying them so we could go back home for that day and study. She finished by saying we should pass by her street once every two weeks and she would buy one plastic bag of tomatoes from us.

That street became our favourite, and more people started buying from us on that street. Some days all of our tomatoes would get finished just on that one street and we would go back to pick up more tomatoes. My brother and I worked for the whole day and some days we came back just before dusk often with one or two bags left. We had found out that it was more difficult to sell just one or two bags, so sometimes we just walked home slowly, so we could get there when dinner was ready. The six of us lived in one room – my sister, three brothers, as well as my mother and my father. The room was separated by a curtain to give my mom and dad some privacy. In the evening my dad sat outside until we were all asleep and then he would come into the house and sleep. In the morning he woke up incredibly early to go to work. He was always working. Sometimes he would pick up odd jobs; sometimes he would go away to camp on the roadside as they constructed the roads. When we were not selling tomatoes during the day we spent most of our time outside playing, but my father would stay indoors to avoid being recognized if he was at home during the day.

He had taken to wearing a hat so people could not recognize him. Even though we were far away from Chamini, he still worried he would be identified. He was now on a wanted list on both sides. The Rhodesian forces thought he was still supporting the guerrilla fighters and the freedom fighters thought he had joined the Rhodesian forces and was supplying them with information.

There had been a battle soon after we left Chamini where the freedom fighters were ambushed and a few of them died. During that time one of the locals claimed that he had seen my father at his home during the day and said that my father had sold out the Comrades. However, my father was nowhere near the house, since he was being looked for by the Rhodesian forces. They now believed he was getting medicines for the freedom fighters and running a clinic for them in the bush. None of it was true.

One time, my mother decided to go with us to buy some used shoes at a flea market – Mukambo at Makokoba, a neighbouring area in Bulawayo. In this outdoor market you can to this day buy food, clothes, dried fish, dried meat – anything. It was packed with used clothes, which came from different countries, along with some donated by the well-to-do in the fancy suburbs of Bulawayo. The shoes we had been using had holes in them. When we got to the market, it was very noisy and dirty, things were piled on the ground and in some cases on countertops made of bricks. My mother took us around the mazelike place and we finally found the shoe area. The selling was by negotiation and my mother managed to get us two pairs of shoes for two dollars, a dollar a pair. These were refurbished shoes. You could see the wrinkles on the shoes from previous owner, but the soles were fresh rubber, which normally came from used car tires. That sole made the shoe look new. My brother and I were so excited to get our "new shoes" we literally threw away the ones we had on and wore the new shoes home. I remember the shoes were a little tight on the top, but I was not going to complain. When we got home, I told my father about the tightness. He took the shoes and stuffed them tight with newspapers to stretch them.

One weekend my father came up with a plan to go and check if the house in Chamini was still standing. He took off with one of my uncles and they drove all the way without stopping at any gas station. They carried extra fuel in two twenty-litre cans so as to minimize chances of my dad being seen, though he wore his hat and sunglasses, as always, during that period.

They arrived at the store around midday. The whole area seemed deserted and they pretended to be visitors. My dad walked into the store through the front where the doors had been taken away. The windows were smashed and there were clothes all over – the shop had been heavily vandalized. My uncle stayed outside watching and listening for anybody coming.

As my father went around the back, he found the most brutal thing ever. His favourite dog lay there with a bullet hole through its head. My father got a shovel, quickly dug a hole and buried the dog. After that they left quickly. My father told me he did not know what to make of the situation. He felt whoever killed the dog was ready to kill him too. This was the last time my father made such a daring move. He told himself he would not come back until the war was over.

I started fourth grade while we lived in Bulawayo. I was a small child; I had lost a lot of weight since the war had started. We were not getting enough to eat. My mother struggled to find food and to find the money to keep us in school. We had porridge in the morning, which my sister would make for us before we went to school and then we did not eat until dinnertime when my mother would come back from selling tomatoes.

This was very stressful for our family as we came from a rural area where food was in abundance. In Chamini I could eat fresh corn or watermelons and sometimes you would just pick wild fruits such as guavas and mangoes or sip sweet juices from flowers. During the beginning of summer there were so many wild fruits you never went hungry.

In Bulawayo, my mother would take some of the money from the day's sales of vegetables and buy a piece of meat from the nearby butcher shop that was very close to where she was selling vegetables. Most days we would eat the remaining vegetables that she could not sell. As kids we did not like to eat vegetables – they didn't go well with sadza. However, we did not ever complain about it because we knew that my mother was trying her best.

The most popular dish for the family was pork sausages and vegetables. The sausages were made of leftover pork cuts.

I remember that the casings for the sausages were so thin that every time my mom tried to fry them, the sausages would break apart and end up looking like thin soup. The vegetables were mainly kale, which made it look a lot better. The sausages were always served with sadza.

The place where my mother sold vegetables was not the designated market, and sometimes the municipality police would come and chase all the sellers away. It was five or six women selling tomatoes, green vegetables, sweet potatoes, potatoes, roasted salted peanuts and cabbages. My mother and the other vendors would place a straw mat or old clean newspapers on the ground. The four corners of the newspaper were held down by small rocks to keep the newspaper from flying off in the wind. The tomatoes would be placed on the newspaper in small piles of say four or six for a dollar.

I remember I used to count the number of tomatoes in a dish she could carry on her head. There could be twenty dollars of tomatoes and sometimes it took several days to sell them all. Out of the twenty dollars she would make maybe seven to ten dollars profit. Any tomatoes that did not look good, she used for cooking. My brother and I knew how to grade the tomatoes and we would keep aside the green ones and wait for them to turn bright red. When the tomatoes were all bright red, the race was on to sell them before they got soft and started rotting. We did not have a refrigerator, so the timing for selling all the vegetables had to be perfect otherwise they would go bad.

One day at school, I was so hungry that I fainted. Doing physical education was compulsory – the most common activity was running around the track. This normally happened around midday, towards the end of a school day. I fainted during one physical education period and I was sent to the clinic after I recovered. That day I learnt a huge English word that I will never forget. The nurse was talking to the principal and she said, "He is hypoglycemic." She took a small packet of glucose and put it in water for me to drink.

I went home and looked in the dictionary to find out what "hypoglycemic" meant. At first, I could not find it in the dictionary because of how it is spelled. I asked my older sister, who told me to try looking for a word that started with "hy," and she went on to explain that some English words are of Greek and Latin origin. I did not understand what that meant at that time, but I finally found the word in the dictionary. I finally knew what it meant. My brother and I had fun with the word and whenever we were hungry after that incident, we used to say to our mother that we were "hypo," and she would laugh.

In Mpopoma primary school there was a program for half a pint of milk in the morning every day for a week for a dollar, but my mother did not have this money. By now my oldest brother was living with friends he had met at work as it was too crowded at the house where we were staying. When my oldest brother heard that I fainted in school, he came over one night to talk to my mother and he decided to send two dollars every week from the little money he earned from his part-time job. He came over every weekend to give my brother Paul and I a dollar each for the week so we could get some milk. For a dollar, the school provided 350 millilitres of milk; without the money you did not get anything. The dollar was for five pints per week. The price was heavily subsided by the government.

My father kept away from the house. He would meet with my mother in a secret location to give her some money when he could. Sometimes my mum would bring him food for a week, such as cooked dried vegetables called "mufushwa." The dried vegetables were prepared using an ancient way of preserving. First you boil the vegetables, often greens, in salted water, then you sun-dry the greens. Sun-dried tomatoes are prepared the same way. Once dry, the vegetables are good for a very long period and no refrigeration is required. You can either eat the vegetables as a snack or you can add hot water to soften and use them as relish.

My father was still working as a dump truck driver, also called a tipper, driving for a road construction company. This was a perfect job as it made it hard for anyone trying to locate him to find him. The company he worked for specialized in making new roads. My father would send my oldest brother with money to give to my mother for rent when he couldn't come. Sometimes he would show up in the middle of the night to see us, bringing some food and money. He would wake us up and stay for an hour or so then disappear into the night. Most of the time after he left, I could not sleep, wondering where he would have gone. Only my mother knew. I later learnt that he was staying with a relative who lived just on the outskirts of the city when he was in town.

My father knew he was still being looked for by the Rhodesian forces. He had heard it from someone who was in the Rhodesian forces who said that he saw my father's name on a list of people who were wanted. Whether this was true or not it was cause for concern for my family. Those who worked for the Rhodesian forces treated the war like a normal job. They were paid and had pension benefits; they had days off and could go home to see their families and move around in town like normal people on their days off. However, people in the towns always looked at them as bad people for working with the current government, killing their own people. But no one had the nerve to approach a guy working as a soldier to say anything.

The soldiers themselves would leak information about potential attacks on some rural areas, most of which was false, but these Rhodesian soldiers were trying to get acceptance from people as good guys. My father decided at that time that even the town was dangerous. If he was noticed by one of these Rhodesian soldiers, they could come and pick him up. He decided to make sure he did not stay in one place for too long.

The thing I learnt about life is that we worry too much about what we own. Life is about having fun and enjoying every minute of it in bad or good times, though I know this is easier said than done. Some of my best years were during the times we were suffering. I saw this again during the pandemic. I heard people talk about how it was the most time they had ever had with their family.

My mum would buy us only essential clothes and shoes. I grew up during a time when shoes were optional in the rural areas. Coming to school in your uniform shirt and pants was the only requirement. Not wearing shoes was not a measurement of poverty, it was normal. Our feet are designed with a thick skin on the bottom and with time the skin hardens enough that you can walk on gravel roads and not feel any pain.

But in town it was different. A uniform meant from head to toe, including shoes. She needed to buy my older sister, my young brother Paul and I new shoes for school one year. She decided to buy us used shoes from Mukambo, Bulawayo's oldest and biggest flea market. She bought us three pairs as she was ordering more vegetables for the following week. She did not have much time as she had to walk from the market home since she did not want to pay for a bus.

When she got home, she gave us the shoes and I remember noticing immediately that mine were girls' shoes. They were flat schoolgirls' shoes with no laces, just a small crossover buckle on the top. I knew she could not take them back and if I did not wear them, she would have lost two dollars. I told my mum that I would wear them until they were torn, and I wore them with pride.

When my teacher asked me why I was wearing those shoes, I told her that my mum bought them for me. And I told her they were the right colour so I did not see any problem with it. The teacher said she liked my attitude and that if anyone ever said anything to me, to let her know. Some people laughed at me during break but I did not care. Even some girls would say directly, "Do you know that those are girls' shoes?" To which I would reply, "They are amazingly comfortable. Do you want to try them?" I do not know now how I had the courage to do that.

I did not speak good IsiNdebele, which is the language spoken in Matabeleland, the region where Bulawayo is located, so when some people would stare at my feet and say something in IsiNdebele, I did not care to find out what they said. I thought to myself it's even better that I do not understand the language. None of this bothered me; my revenge was in class. I did well with homework and at the end of semester exams I received incredibly good grades in Math, English and Science, so it sort of cancelled out. After that some people joked that my secret was wearing girls' shoes. After a while no one cared about my brother Paul and I wearing girls' shoes. There was only one bully who I had to report to my class teacher for he would not stop teasing me. Every time he saw me in the hallway, he would follow me until I got to my next class saying, in my native language, Shona, that I was making Shona people look bad.

My sister Evelyn went to a different primary school, while my brother Paul and I went to Mpumelelo Primary School in Mpopoma. We always wished that our sister would go to the same school so we could have protection. My brother and I were known to be poor – some students in the neighbourhood had seen us selling tomatoes and some knew our mum sold tomatoes by the side of the road. I remember in our selling adventures we found out where a couple of teachers lived. The one thing about people knowing that you are poor is sometimes you then know that no matter what you do, they think you are going to die poor. They feel sorry for you for a minute and then move on with their lives. You get a second of thought, if you are lucky, then you are no longer a person to them. They cancel you though they do not see how you are going to come out. People talk of cancel culture these days as if it's a new concept, but it was always there. How many times have you seen some poor African child on TV in a commercial for contributions to go and help hungry children in Africa. For years I have seen the picture of almost the same kid. Has no one asked where they are now? That hungry child, how is he doing now? Has he grown up and if so, did his life improve? Or is he dead? Strangely enough, when you are poor not many people ask how you got into that situation. What I found interesting was how people cancel you very quickly without knowing the story.

My family could not tell the story, even if we were asked. We were not supposed to talk about it. My father was basically a wanted man and my mum told us never to talk about where we were from and how we ended up poor. Funny enough, no one ever asked.

In my head, I occasionally asked myself why we were suffering. I would think about our home, about my friends in school in the rural areas where no one judged us for not wearing shoes, where food was not always about money, where fruit was picked off a tree and not bought from the side of the road. The thought would make me happy, but most of the time the happiness would be cut short by remembering where I was. Sometimes the sound of a car horn would startle me and I would suddenly realize that I had to focus on this new jungle of cars, bicycles and buses. The daydreaming always ended with me thinking of the day when the end of the gun barrel was in my face, that confusing night when the Rhodesian forces posed as freedom fighters. Sometimes it was just flashbacks of the night we escaped the war and walked to Muzvondiwa to take a bus to Mashaba.

My parents prayed a lot. They pretty much gave us hope through their prayers, which carried my family though the difficult time. I grew up singing church songs. I still remember some of the hymns from the church. My brother Paul and I used to sing some of those songs regularly.

As a kid I felt that I did not have all the stuff that other people had, but I was happy. I always thought of everything that was happening as temporary and that one day, when the war was over, all these people that were looking at us weird, as very poor people, would know that we were not so poor, that we had goats, cattle and a home to live in. My mother and father always reminded us that we had a home and that one day, when the war was over, we were going to go back.

CHAPTER 4
FLEEING TO HARARE

Though my father had a job in Bulawayo, the money was not enough. Just paying rent and food was a challenge for my family. The vegetable business that my mother was running provided most of the money we needed to buy day-to-day food. My big brother Wilbert, who was now living with his friends, used to come by and give my mom a few dollars for food when he could. But my father was thinking of finding a better place for us since the six of us were still cramped in one room, with only a curtain to provide my father and mother some privacy, or peace if my father wanted to rest after a long week of driving.

One afternoon Abbas, my father's nephew, came to the house looking for my father. He told my mother that it was particularly important that my father get in touch with him. Abbas was exceptionally light-skinned, with curly hair, and he spoke both Shona and English, which always amazed me. If you did not know him, you would think that he was white. He had long blond hair that he trimmed only in the front – the back of his head was full of hair. Given that my hair is short and curly African hair, I was always fascinated by the way his hair looked. I wondered to myself how a man so light-skinned could speak the Shona native language so fluently.

His mother was Black and of the same totem as my dad so we called her auntie. Given that Abbas had never seen his father he took seriously the fact that my dad was his uncle. Before the war he would drive to the rural areas some weekends to come and spend time with my dad. Most of the time he was fixing my dad's car. As with all or most people like him in Zimbabwe, he knew more about cars. It's just the way it is – most light-skinned people in Zimbabwe know how to fix cars.

He was always close to my father. When he used to come and see us in the rural areas, he'd sit around with my father at night drinking bottled beers. So when he had trouble with his wife, she would come over to my dad and tell him all about it. Things like, "Abbas is not coming back home until very late at night" or "Abbas is drinking too much."

The funniest of all was when she said he hangs around with his friends all the time, to which Abbas said to my dad, "Uncle, even if it was you, if you were there you would have hung around with them too! They had so much beer I couldn't leave!" He added, "Even if my wife was there, she would not leave, so I'm not sure why she's telling you all this. Maybe she's jealous that I was having such a good time." Saying it in our native language just made it even more funny.

A couple of days after Abbas's visit, my father got us all together as family and told us that our big brother Wilbert had been forced into the army. The Rhodesian army was now conscripting all public servants – Black men, Coloured men and white men – to serve in the army for one year. This was a shift from the selected conscription that had happened before this. The recruits got some training, though it was not really equivalent to the normal combat soldier training. It was more like the national security/guard program and those who were called up were given jobs as drivers or guards. In some cases these call-up recruits were used to go and collect dead soldiers after a battle. My brother wanted to be a veterinarian, so he had found a job as a laboratory assistant at the government-run veterinary services. He was considered a public servant and he was then forced to go into the army.

My father considered having him run away to the UK like many other young men, but the consequences of getting caught were serious – he would be imprisoned. My brother decided he would go – since he had a driver's licence and formal high school education, he would not be a foot soldier, he would only be driving the army trucks. His boss at the clinic, who was white, told him that he was going to be fine and that when he came back, he would continue with his training. My brother really wanted to be a veterinarian and this was a pathway for him to achieve his dream. There were not that many Black animal doctors and he was going to be one of a few. After his boss gave him courage by telling him he would be fine and he found out he would not be going far away from the city, he agreed.

My brother prefers not to talk about what the job was when he was called up towards the end of the war. I know at one time he mentioned that he was driving Crocodile troop carriers, which was the Rhodesian forces' preferred reinforced metal armoured vehicle, in the Shurugwi rural area just south of Gweru. This area is approximately fifty kilometres away from our home area in Chamini. He told me that he was so scared that he would be seen driving the Rhodesian trucks by someone from our rural area and the whole family would be killed for it.

Most disturbing was the fact that some of my cousins were fighting the war from the other side with the freedom fighters. Even worse, my father was known in the freedom fighter community, so information that my brother had been called up was dangerous and driving the army trucks was dangerous. The whole thing did not make sense to me towards the end. Why the fighting, the suffering? For three years of my early childhood all I thought about was survival as we moved from place to place. I felt like our life had been turned upside down. I could not figure it out. All my father did was set up a shop to support his family, my family. Why did the war come to our home? I did not understand the whole idea of the liberation struggle. All the time, I would wonder when it would end. My parents told us constantly that one day we would go back home.

Abbas had also been called up, and one night he came to tell my father that he had seen my father's name on another list of people wanted by the Rhodesian forces. That night my mum prepared our small bags just in case we had to move again.

The list was supposed to be for the people that the army wanted to kill and eliminate, including some small businessmen in the rural areas who they thought were enablers of the freedom fighters. Whether the list existed or not no one will ever know. After the war was over there was a rumour that it was the Rhodesian forces' idea to eliminate all shops in the rural area so the freedom fighters would starve and come out of the mountains. When any of the businessmen were found they would vanish forever.

That night my father told us that he was going to leave Bulawayo and that he would get in touch with us when he got someplace safe. He left the same day in the middle of the night. He later told us that he spent the whole day on the street then took the midnight train the next night and headed to Harare, the capital city. Harare is way bigger than Bulawayo and finding a Black man in Harare is like finding a needle in a haystack.

On the train my father found out that the Rhodesian forces were using the same train to move from town to town. My father sat in a corner with his hat over his face, pretending to sleep. He said at one point a group of soldiers came to sit in his coach and he leaned backwards and put his hat over his head so no one would see his face. This was from Kwekwe to Kadoma, so the entire journey he pretended to be sleeping. The Rhodesian forces and police were everywhere and as my father was already on the watchlist, he knew he was going to be killed if they found him.

As the war progressed people started to sell each other out for food or money. Some people would trade information to the army; the rumour was that in most cases it was about selling the location of freedom fighters. Some told the freedom fighters about others conspiring with Rhodesian soldiers. Many reported business owners for their involvement with either group so they could be let off the hook from questions. The punishment for being found in support of one side by the other, be it the Rhodesian forces or freedom fighters, was death.

My father told us after the war that he would go for days without sleep, only taking a quick nap here and there. He knew his life was in danger. My father lost weight and he was permanently wearing a hat, which made him look older and different. He never stopped to teach us about life, though every chance he had he told us to stay in school and work hard no matter what happened. He was still reading. He read the paper every day and listened to Radio Mozambique, which talked about the war from the freedom fighters' perspective. I still remember the broadcast would come on at six o'clock in the evening and when the broadcast was over you'd hear the words "A luta continua," which is Portuguese for "The struggle continues." My father would also listen to the local Rhodesian news, so he knew what was going on from both sides.

My father was a voracious reader. He would not miss a day of the local paper on top of any other book he found. His English was impeccable. He spoke English as if he was born speaking the language. He liked to replace simple words with new words that he would learn from his extensive reading and he would ask us what we thought the word meant. I remember him using the words "flabbergasted" and "exacerbate." Once I knew the meaning of them, I started using the words too. I remember I wrote an essay once when I was in seventh grade and I sprinkled in some of the words my father had taught us. I got the highest mark and the teacher read it to the whole class and sent it to other teachers to read. I was excited and the teacher said to my father, "The apple does not fall too far from the tree."

CHAPTER 5
GOING BACK TO CHAMINI

When the war was over and the freedom fighters had won the elections, my father was excited and happy. We were all alive and now he could get his property back.

The first thing my father did was look for the war reparation offices where people went to claim for their losses and injuries caused by the war. Weeks later, after days of visiting the new government offices, my father was told that he could not get any money because no one in the family was physically injured or killed. He was told that loss of property did not qualify him for any reparation money. My father sent for someone to take pictures of our destroyed property, the store, our old destroyed car, our home. He explained that the freedom fighters had told him that all the goods they were taking from his store would be replaced. My father talked about how his family was suffering due to a war that he did not ask for; how our lives had been impacted. He was told that what the freedom fighters said was not true and that everyone in the rural areas suffered somehow but that did not qualify everyone to get more from the government and besides, the government did not have that kind of money.

It was devastating for my father and mother. All the property that they had worked hard to get was gone, destroyed during the war. In the rural areas a person with no cows, goats, pigs or livestock was regarded as poor. We were, at this point, poor.

I remember my father coming back home saying that what we were told was all lies. Nobody was going to get a cent for the losses incurred during the war. All of the freedom fighters who had demanded my father give them goods and had promised payment had now disappeared or had died in the war.

But my father and mother were determined to go back home and rebuild. Living in the city was very tough for our family – we were used to staying in the rural areas where you paid no rent, no water bill, no electricity bill. One day my father told us that he was going to quit his job and we were all going to go back home. I was getting a little confused by then, not knowing what to expect. I did not want to go back, fearing what I had experienced in Chamini, but my parents were very excited about this occasion.

When the day came, my father went to collect his old van, a Datsun 1500, and we packed up and left the city, ready to travel three hundred kilometres back to the rural area. It was a Sunday morning. My sister Evelyn, the one who comes before me, woke up early to clean up the house in Harare.

My sister likes everything very clean. If she polished the floor and you stepped into the house with your shoes, she would follow the sneaker tracks to your room to find you and tell you to take your shoes off immediately. I was always in trouble with my sister for walking into the room after she'd cleaned it and for leaving books everywhere. She would go behind me and pick up all the books and then bring them to me and show me as she shouted at me not to be like a pig.

On this day, even as we were leaving the house in Harare, my sister was cleaning so that the new people that would come in to occupy the house would find it clean. While everybody else was loading the car, she was cleaning the windows and the bathrooms and the kitchen. I remember my dad saying to her, "Leave this alone. We are going back home; this will be someone else's problem." She finally dropped the little rag she was holding in her hand for cleaning the windows, but I could see that she could not leave the house like that. She felt like it was still dirty.

It was about mid-morning when we finally got into the car. I still remember how the air was so clean as we drove into the countryside going towards Norton. Norton is a farming area, always green with different crops, from corn to potatoes. The van had a front bench seat where my mother sat while my dad drove the car. In between the front and the truck bed was a window we could look through to see the road ahead. We entertained ourselves in the back of the van by singing and playing games such as name the next town or name the next river.

My mom had cooked rice and chicken for the trip, which was a food eaten on special occasions like Christmas. My father parked the van halfway to Chamini in a rest area at the side of the road and we stopped to eat. It was like a celebration that we had all survived the war. It felt good that there was no more war and that we could finally go back to the place we called home. We knew a lot of people and families had been lost during the war, but we were all alive.

My father's van was not the fastest. I think we were travelling at maybe eighty kilometres an hour or less all the way from Harare to Zvishavane. The whole trip, including stops, took eight hours for a distance of about three hundred kilometres. The funny thing is that journey can be done now in four hours, maybe three and half.

CHAPTER 6
LIFE AFTER THE WAR

When we got back home to Chamini, we found out that all the buildings were burnt down and only the brick walls of the house had survived the fire. Some roofs that had been covered by metal sheets had a couple of them still hanging loosely over the half-burnt trusses made of wooden poles. Because most houses were thatched, they were very easy to burn. But my mom always took in serious things and turned them into something livable. We got there late in the afternoon and the whole family worked to remove the debris and garbage to clean rooms for us to sleep in.

Although the round mud-and-pole houses may seem funny, I can tell you there are several advantages to living in these kinds of houses in this region. When it is hot the grass allows for the rising hot air to escape freely, leaving the inside of the thatched house cooler than outside. In the period from June to July, which is what people regard as winter, temperatures fall to ten degrees Celsius, but the clay walls of the mud-and-pole huts provide adequate thermal insulation to stop the cold air entering the hut. On the roof, the dry grass soaks up the moisture in the air and expands to close the gaps between the grass straws, improving heat retention. One thing I know for sure is the temperature in a mud-and-pole house is always naturally comfortable.

By the time the war was over, my brother and I were older, however, we still went out and looked for some plastic bags to make a soccer ball. The whole place had changed and the quietness was a little bit eerie. The people had changed their behaviour too. It was different. However, the sound of cowbells could be heard across the plains like before. The one thing that the war had taught us was to be united as a family, to help my mother whenever she needed help. As kids we learned how to cook for the family. We learned how to work and look for money for the family. We learned that you always stand by your family and that family matters more than anything else. We learned that our parents loved us.

We lived in the building with no roof for months. My father used to get us to recite "Twinkle, twinkle, little star." It felt magical as he taught us outside at the fire in the middle of the yard at night. This type of fire outside is normally for men and boys only and it is called "Dare." My father was different; he allowed my sister to come over and join us in listening to stories and learning about the culture. We roasted corn to eat while we waited for the dinner my mum was cooking in the kitchen.

In the old days no boys were allowed in the kitchen while the mother and girls were cooking there. The mother's job was to teach the young girls to cook the traditional food and teach them how to serve the food, in preparation for when they got married. In my family anyone could learn how to cook. I remember my mother teaching me how to cook eggs mixed with vegetables to be served with sadza in times when meat was scarce. When I look back, I realize she was cooking scrambled eggs mixed with greens. If done properly with salt, the only seasoning she used, it is very tasty and healthy.

My dad enjoyed telling stories. In African cultures there are many folk stories relating to animals and nature. The stories taught us life lessons, about our culture and how to coexist with the natural environment. But the stories my father told were mainly geared towards how to live in the community and contribute to society. Some stories were about bravery, these were stories of the heroes that used to roam the countryside long ago. Most stories started with "Paivapo," which means "There was once . . ." It was often two animals. I found out that the stories I was particularly interested in were about my father's life as a young boy. He told us how he moved from his home area, how he met our mother, how he and my mother managed to save money and start a shop. How his big brother taught him how to drive and how his brother encouraged him to go to school. During their time they were important people in the area. Back then, driving a car was not common for young Black men. It meant freedom.

One famous story is centred on the baboon and the rabbit. There was once the rabbit and the baboon. The two were bored and hungry – it was a time of drought. These two were friends, but the baboon wanted to eat the rabbit and so he came up with a game to play. He said, "Hey, let's play a game. We'll jump into the pot of water on the fire. As soon you feel the heat call out, 'I am getting hot,' then I will pull you out." So the baboon went in first and sat inside the pot of water on the fire. As the water got hot, he said, "Hey, I am getting hot," so the rabbit helped him out. Then it was the rabbit's turn and so the rabbit jumped in. He sat there for a minute and by then the water was getting hot, so the rabbit called out, "The water is getting hot! Take me out." However, the baboon closed the lid. The rabbit kept calling, "Please get me out," until he was cooked into soft meat. And the baboon replied, "Tsiramo tidye nyama," which means "Burn in there so I can eat meat." And so the rabbit was cooked inside the pot and the baboon ate the rabbit for food.

This story was told several times and it was meant to warn young boys to be careful who you play with, for some of your friends can get you into trouble.

There are many more stories based on animals, where they are friends, which tell us the dangers that animals would go through. Such stories were linked to how people live together and how nature is the backbone of human survival. They taught about respect for other living creatures, such as not to kill an animal if you are not going to eat it. And that if you like an animal for food, you should treat the animal with respect for it provides you with food.

One thing that is beautiful about sleeping in a house with no roof is that you get to see the sky every day. There is nothing as good as falling asleep gazing at the stars. Sometimes I would try to count the bright stars until I fell asleep. Sometimes I would make a wish after I saw a shooting star. I believe some of the wishes came true, as some of the wishes were things like one day I would like to sleep in a house with a roof on. Of course, my parents were working vigorously to get us a roof before the weather started to get cold and the rains arrived.

A few days after we came back, the villagers gathered at the store and decided to help my family settle back in. Some gave us some cornmeal, some brought biltong, some just volunteered to go and look for the grass for thatching the roof. You would never see this kind of behaviour in the city. This is why my dad came back to Chamini. It felt like home.

My parents repaired the walls with some clay mud used for making bricks, as our old neighbours brought grass for thatching our roof. With their help, we soon had a roof over our house. We only spent about two months sleeping in a house without a roof, but by the time we got the roof on our house I was already used to it and it did not bother me at all. I actually felt strange when we finally got a roof. I felt claustrophobic and it took some time to get used to sleeping inside a roofed house. Sometimes the beauty about being a kid is everything seems to be an adventure.

We did not have any cattle remaining at home when we returned, since with no one to look after the cattle when we escaped, the cattle just roamed the land. We were told by a neighbour that one or two of them were slaughtered to feed the freedom fighters.

One day my father and I went out talking to the neighbours

and other people from the area, looking for our cattle. We managed to find two cattle that were being kept by one of the villagers. The man told my dad that he knew we were going to come back – he had told other villagers that it was just a matter of time. He said that he had dreamt that my dad was not dead but that he was going to come back and rebuild his home. I was moved listening to the old man as he spoke to my father. He was one of those wise old villagers who always had that foresight about life. He told my dad that all his kids were going to be great. He told me that I was going to go places.

The man gave my dad two bags of corn and he asked us to wait for the cattle to come back from the grazing area and then we could have our two cows back. My father and I were excited to see the black-and-white heifer that was now much bigger than we left it. Apparently, he kept the cows very well, taking them for good grazing and taking them to get water by the river. My father told the neighbour that he was going to pay him back for keeping his cattle. I remember the old man saying that that's all he could do for his friend and he was happy my father was back. He would help rebuild the store.

When we moved back it was the beginning of summertime and hot, so we could not plant anything for food. The food we brought from the city, and the gifts from neighbours, did not last long. The money my father had saved working in Harare quickly ran out, spent on building materials to repair the home. The school was also rebuilding at that time. Since my father had a car, he was asked to help with bringing nails, windows and door handles for the school from Zvishavane.

My father's car was the only means of transport for all the locals to go to town. People would come over to the house and ask him when he was going to town and then they would plan their trips around that time. He would get to town and drop them off at the main bus station in Zvishavane, Mandava. There they would find buses to go wherever they were going. Some would opt to come back with him at the end of the day so he would tell them to wait at a certain time on the side of the main road leading out of town near a hospital called "White hospital," which was the location of the last station coming out of Zvishavane. The town itself was very small and so you could walk to anywhere to get what you needed. Rural people did not and still do not use taxis; they are used to walking. They walked to various places buying things for their families. Some would be going to the hospital. I was surprised when I went back recently to find people still using this location for hitchhiking.

My father decided to look for a job at the school as a teacher so he could get an income to support the family as we rebuilt the home and store. Luckily, he got the job to be a teacher for grade six. My father instantly became popular at the school because of how well he spoke and taught English and Math. He was well known for his eloquent English and for encouraging students in school. Some students would follow him and walk with him as he came home just to learn something else from the old man.

It was weird for me to see my father teaching. By then I was in grade seven and it was odd to hear my father teaching next door, as it was a voice I had heard all my life. Sometimes I would hear him telling the kids in the class his folk stories. Our class was more serious and quiet because grade seven in Zimbabwe is the grade before you go to high school, commonly known in those parts of the world as secondary school. So most of the time our class was quiet and doing our work and you could hear other classes singing and practising English words. Grade seven pretty much decides for you if you are going to go away from home to secondary school or if you would be stuck repeating the grade or just not bother trying again, as some did, and just become one of the local labourers to someone in the cornfields.

The year seemed to go by very fast and I finally finished grade seven. The waiting period for the exam results seemed very long.

After the war the new government introduced new secondary schools called Upper Tops. The schools were introduced as part of a new program that was dubbed "education for all." The program was geared towards rural areas and was meant to bring secondary schools to the parts of the country that didn't have any, but the schools faced shortages in equipment, especially for the science labs. I was determined to do sciences and to not miss anything. I wanted to learn as much as I could, so I did not want to go to the Upper Tops. I wrote a letter while I waited for my results and asked my brother if I could stay with him in Bulawayo so I could attend more established schools in town.

Although my brother was starting his life, he opted to take me and my sister Evelyn with him to the city where he lived and vouched that he would let us have a better education, and he did just that. My brother Wilbert, the first-born in our family, used to tell me that he would sacrifice anything to have all his siblings go to school. When I was living with him, he told me the lesson he got from our father, which was that "if I did not help my brothers, it would mean that I would be taking care of you for the rest of my life." He added that our father had told him that his family would come to his house and stay there, borrow or steal his clothes and he would be supporting them for the rest of his life. My brother told me the thought of him being the only one successful in the family and the rest of us bothering him for the rest of his life was frightening to him, so he decided early on that he would help everyone go to school. Then we could fend for ourselves in the future.

As soon as you finished school and started working, you were supposed to help the younger siblings with school fees to go through their education. My sister Nicky, who is the second-born of the family, followed suit. As soon as she started teaching, she was helping us younger ones too. The structure that my father had set up helped us all to go to school. I am forever grateful to my big brother for giving me the chance to get a decent education.

I passed my grade seven exams and moved on to another phase of my life, living with my brother in Bulawayo as a secondary/high school student. Although the war was over my brother Wilbert was just finishing off his training as a veterinary laboratory technician. He was still struggling to make ends meet and he had to take care of me and my sister Evelyn; however, he managed to send us to school. My father occasionally sent him money after selling his crop.

At this time my father was concentrating more on his second wife's kids, who were still young, and so for me and my siblings my brother and mom took care of things.

I have not talked much about my mom; however, if I was to point out the person that kept the whole family together and if you ask any of my siblings, the answer would unequivocally be our mother. The way I see it, my father was the leader in thinking about ideas to make money and my mother was the one who made it happen and made sure that the family stayed together. She taught us respect for each other. She was the like the CEO of the home. She has a wonderful ability to keep the peace and a can-do attitude.

EPILOGUE

I still remember everything like it was yesterday. I hold on to that thought, hoping that as I grow older, I will still remember every bit of it. However, I know my memories will start to fade as I grow older. In this, my first book, I decided to write about what I saw as a boy growing up in a war-torn country, to preserve my memories of my early childhood.

I moved to the USA in 1999 when I was twenty-eight years of age. In Zimbabwe I had worked and achieved a journeyman certificate to become an electrician. However, becoming an electrician was a stepping stone for me to go to university and attain an electrical engineering degree. I remember one day during my final year of apprenticeship, we were sitting outside at the back of the electrical shop at Sable Chemical Industries in Kwekwe and one of the senior guys, who had been working there for years as a semi-skilled electrician, asked me the most common question you get asked in your final year. He asked me, "What is your plan when you finish your apprenticeship training?"

To which I responded, "I want to go abroad and do my electrical engineering degree."

He then responded with a puzzled expression on his face, "How are you going to do that? With the pay you are getting and even when you finish it's impossible to raise that kind of money." I am happy to announce I fulfilled that dream.

ACKNOWLEDGEMENTS

Thank you to my dad and mom, my brothers and sisters who helped me along the way. Without them, I would not be here authoring this book.

Thank you to my supportive wife and my kids for holding on through all the challenging times we went through, spending so much time at work, working long hours in various jobs.

I will forever cherish our experiences.

George Makonese Matuvi grew up in Chamini, a rural area in the district of Zvishavane, in Zimbabwe, where he was surrounded by mountains and developed a love of both soccer and books. He is currently an electrical engineer and runs a small consulting company. *The War as I Saw It: In Rhodesia, Now Zimbabwe, Through the Eyes of a Black Boy* is his first book. He lives in Hamilton, Ontario, with his family.